Do it

The Lazy Way

alpha books

S0-BCT-235

1. Compare scholarships using your computer.

2. Check your bank accounts over the phone.

3. File your taxes electronically.

4. Create a "tax receipt" drawer to stockpile receipts until tax time.

5. Trade stocks online.

*One luxurious
bubble bath*

*Access to most comfortable
chair and favorite TV show*

*One half-hour massage
(will need to recruit spouse, child, friend)*

*Time to recline and listen to a favorite cd
(or at least one song)*

cut

6. Have your tax refund, paycheck, and Social Security deposited automatically into your checking account.

7. Order your Social Security records over the phone.

8. Let your CD roll over automatically.

9. Apply for college electronically.

10. Put money into your mutual fund via automatic deduction from your bank account.

COUPON

COUPON

COUPON

COUPON

cut

Handle Your Money

Handle Your Money

Carol Turkington and
Sarah Young Fisher

Macmillan • USA

I dedicate this book to my son, Rob. He has a gift of finding the easiest path to achieve his goal.

—With love, Mom

Macmillan Publishing books may be purchased for business or sales promotional use. For information please write: Special Markets Department, Macmillan Publishing USA, 1633 Broadway, New York, NY 10019.

International Standard Book Number: 0-02-862632-X
Library of Congress Catalog Card Number: 98-88080

99 98   8 7 6 5 4 3 2 1

Interpretation of the printing code: The rightmost number of the first series of numbers is the year of the book's printing; the rightmost number of the second series of numbers is the number of the book's printing. For example, a printing code of 98-1 shows that the first printing occurred in 1998.

Book Design: Madhouse Studios

Manufactured in the United States of America

10 9 8 7 6 5 4 3 2 1

Page creation by Carrie Allen and Heather Pope.

You Don't Have to Feel Guilty Anymore!

IT'S O.K. TO DO IT *THE LAZY WAY*!

It seems every time we turn around, we're given more responsibility, more information to absorb, more places we need to go, and more numbers, dates, and names to remember. Both our bodies and our minds are already on overload. And we know what happens next—cleaning the house, balancing the checkbook, and cooking dinner get put off until "tomorrow" and eventually fall by the wayside.

So let's be frank—we're all starting to feel a bit guilty about the dirty laundry, stacks of ATM slips, and Chinese take-out. Just thinking about tackling those terrible tasks makes you exhausted, right? If only there were an easy, effortless way to get this stuff done! (And done right!)

There is—*The Lazy Way*! By providing the pain-free way to do something—including tons of shortcuts and time-saving tips, as well as lists of all the stuff you'll ever need to get it done efficiently—*The Lazy Way* series cuts through all of the time-wasting thought processes and laborious exercises. You'll discover the secrets of those who have figured out *The Lazy Way*. You'll get things done in half the time it takes the average person—and then you will sit back and smugly consider those poor suckers who haven't discovered *The Lazy Way* yet. With *The Lazy Way,* you'll learn how to put in minimal effort and get maximum results so you can devote your attention and energy to the pleasures in life!

THE LAZY WAY PROMISE

Everyone on *The Lazy Way* staff promises that, if you adopt *The Lazy Way* philosophy, you'll never break a sweat, you'll barely lift a finger, you won't put strain on your brain, and you'll have plenty of time to put up your feet. We guarantee you will find that these activities are no longer hardships, since you're doing them *The Lazy Way*. We also firmly support taking breaks and encourage rewarding yourself (we even offer our suggestions in each book!). With *The Lazy Way*, the only thing you'll be overwhelmed by is all of your newfound free time!

THE LAZY WAY SPECIAL FEATURES

Every book in our series features the following sidebars in the margins, all designed to save you time and aggravation down the road.

- **"Quick n' Painless"**—shortcuts that get the job done fast.
- **"You'll Thank Yourself Later"**—advice that saves time down the road.
- **"A Complete Waste of Time"**—warnings that spare countless headaches and squandered hours.
- **"If You're So Inclined"**—optional tips for moments of inspired added effort.
- **"The Lazy Way"**—rewards to make the task more pleasurable.

If you've either decided to give up altogether or have taken a strong interest in the subject, you'll find information on hiring outside help with "How to Get Someone Else to Do It" as well as further reading recommendations in "If You Want to Learn More, Read These." In addition, there's an only-what-you-need-to-know glossary of terms and product names ("If You Don't Know What It Means/Does, Look Here") as well as "It's Time for Your Reward"—fun and relaxing ways to treat yourself for a job well done.

With *The Lazy Way* series, you'll find that getting the job done has never been so painless!

Series Editor
Amy Gordon

Editorial Director
Gary Krebs

Director of Creative Services
Michele Laseau

Cover Designer
Michael Freeland

Managing Editor
Robert Shuman

Production Editor
Donna Wright

What's in This Book

I know what you're saying: "Me, scrimp and save?" My response to you would be, "No, not really." I'll show you all of the tricks to a balanced budget—and some savings put away as well— without a degree in accounting.

With these worksheets and checklists, you'll be well on your way to sorting out your finances.

Check here to tap into the information that will make managing your money a breeze.

Just a little organization will maximize your success, minimize your confusion.

There's always a way to cut costs without cutting out style. Here's how.

Having Nightmares About Your Finances? Don't Worry! You're Not Alone!

It's April 14. You're surrounded by records, canceled checks, and receipts—at least, the ones you were able to find crumpled up in that shoe box under the bed with the dust bunnies.

It's too late to stash some of your money in an IRA. Your checkbook hasn't been balanced in months, there are at least three months' worth of unrecorded ATM slips underneath your car seats, and you don't even want to think about what you and your husband are going to retire on. But that's 20 years from now, so you've got plenty of time, right?

Then you remember that's what you said about college when your daughter was born 15 years ago. Now she's a sophomore in high school, and you don't have a clue how you're going to pay for college.

Your heart starts to pound. Maybe you should get another job. How else will you find the money to save, much less invest? But even if you had enough money to invest, how would you know where to put your money? It's all so complicated, and it all takes so much time and effort.

Wrong! Understanding money management basics isn't that complicated, and you'd be surprised how many time-saving tips there are to help you streamline your finances. We take advantage of them all the time: Mortgages are automatically deducted from checking accounts. Deposits to mutual funds are whisked out of our accounts electronically, account balances are checked by phone, and taxes get filed over the telephone lines.

It's neat, it's fast, and it doesn't hurt—because the organized way is the easy way.

So whether you just need to update your money management strategies or you don't know a stock option from a sow's ear, *Handling Your Money The Lazy Way* is your solution to managing your money without having your money manage you. Dust off that checkbook and fire up the computer—we're ready to start managing your money *The Lazy Way*.

And thanks so much to our terrific editor, Alana J. Morgan, for shepharding this book from start to finish.

The Effortless Ledger

Are You Too Lazy to Read About The Effortless Ledger?

1 You'd really like to know when your CD's will roll over, but you haven't seen the paperwork on your investments since your toddler decided to redecorate your office. ☐ yes ☐ no

2 You know that there are people who actually understand the tax office, but who knows where to find an honest tax preparer anyway. ☐ yes ☐ no

3 You'd like to take out a life insurance policy but can't make heads or tails out of all the options your insurance agent would like you to buy. ☐ yes ☐ no

Chapter one

Worksheets to Whiz Through

Before you gasp in distress at all of the blank spaces to fill in, sit back and have a nice cup of tea! These worksheets are here to help you use the information you'll get after reading the upcoming chapters on managing your money. Once you know what to put into these forms, you'll find that you've saved yourself countless hours for years to come!

Monthly Budget

Income	Jan.	Feb.	March	April	May	
Wages						
Income						
Dividends						
Interest						
Rent						
Trust						
Investments						
Alimony						

	June	July	Aug.	Sept.	Oct.	Nov.	Dec.

QUICK **n** PAINLESS

Why spend countless hours searching through all of your files when a sample form like this can put everything at your fingertips?

NET WORTH WORKSHEET

Assets

Bonds	$_____
Cash Accounts	$_____
Cash Value Life Insurance	$_____
Certificates of Deposit	$_____
Limited Partnerships	$_____
Mutual Funds	$_____
Savings Bonds	$_____
Stocks	$_____
Tax Refunds	$_____
Treasury Bills	$_____
Subtotal	$_____
Personal Property	
Businesses	$_____
Cars	$_____
Personal Property	$_____
Subtotal	$_____
Real Estate	
Income Property	$_____
Mortgages Owed	$_____
Residence	$_____
Vacation Home	$_____
Subtotal	$_____
Retirement	
Annuities	$_____
IRAs	$_____
Keogh Accounts	$_____
Pensions	$_____
Subtotal	$_____
Total Assets	$_____

Liabilities

Alimony	$_____
Child Support	$_____
Personal Loans	$_____
Subtotal	$_____
Installment Liabilities	
Bank Loans	$_____
Car Loans	$_____
College Loans	$_____
Credit Card Bills	$_____
Furniture Loans	$_____
Home Improvement Loans	$_____
Life Insurance Loans	$_____
Pension Plan Loans	$_____
Subtotal	$_____
Real Estate Liabilities	
Income property	$_____
Residence (Include second mortgage/line of credit)	$_____
Vacation Home	$_____
Subtotal	$_____
Taxes	
Capital Gains Tax	$_____
Income Tax	$_____
Property Tax	$_____
Subtotal	$_____
Other Liabilities	
	$_____
	$_____
Total Assets	$_____
Total Liabilities	$_____
Total Net Worth	$_____

A COMPLETE WASTE OF TIME

The 3 Worst Things to Do When Handling Your Finances:

1. Don't save your receipts.

2. Don't track your expenses.

3. Treat your bank balance as if it were a bottomless well.

CASH ACCOUNTS WORKSHEET

Use this simple form to consolidate all your cash account information—and feel free to make copies if you have more than one account.

Bank name: _____

Type of account: _____

Account # _____

Joint account name: _____

Address: _____

E-mail address: _____

Contact name: _____

Work phone: _____

ATM card #: _____

Location of checkbooks/records: _____

IF YOU'RE SO INCLINED

Use these simple forms to track all of your account information and keep everything in one folder for quick and easy access.

CERTIFICATES OF DEPOSIT WORKSHEET

Use this simple form to consolidate your CD information.

Bank name: _____

Type of account: _____

Account # _____

Name(s) on account: _____

Address: _____

E-mail address: _____

Contact name: _____

Work phone: _____

Principal: $_____

Location of certificate: _____

Date purchased: _____   Maturity date: _____

CHARITABLE DONATIONS RECORD

Use this form to record your donations to charity—at tax time you'll be able to have all your information in one place!

Cash Contributions

Charity	Date	Amount

Noncash Contributions

Charity	Check #	Date	Amount

YOU'LL THANK YOURSELF LATER

By keeping track of your donations as you go, you can cut down your tax preparation time by half!

CAR MAINTENANCE RECORD

Keep track of all your car records here. Keeping all the relevant information in one place makes it that much easier to track your average car expenses.

Car model and make: _____ Year: _____

Service center: _____

Address: _____

Phone: (___)_____ Fax: (___)_____

Mechanic's name: _____

Repairs Done

Date	Odometer Reading	Repair	Cost

Congratulations! You've made sure that your family will know how to take care of you later in life, now treat everyone to an ice cream cone!

The Lazy Way

ADVANCE DIRECTIVE FOR HEALTH CARE DECLARATION

I, [print your name] _____,
being of sound mind, willfully and voluntarily make this declaration to be followed if I become incompetent. This declaration reflects my firm and settled commitment to refuse life-sustaining treatment under the circumstances indicated below.

I direct my attending physician to withhold or withdraw life-sustaining treatment that serves only to prolong the process of my dying, if I should be in a terminal condition or in a state of permanent unconsciousness.

I direct that treatment be limited to measures to keep me comfortable and to relieve pain, including any pain that might occur by withholding or withdrawing life-sustaining treatment.

In addition, if I am in the condition described above, I feel especially strongly about the following forms of treatment [please check one box for each statement, but only if you have a preference at this time]:

I do ☐ do not ☐ want cardiac resuscitation.
I do ☐ do not ☐ want mechanical respiration.
I do ☐ do not ☐ want tube feeding or any other artificial or invasive form of nutrition (food) or hydration (water).
I do ☐ do not ☐ want blood or blood products.
I do ☐ do not ☐ want any form of surgery or invasive diagnostic tests.
I do ☐ do not ☐ want kidney dialysis.
I do ☐ do not ☐ want antibiotics.

I realize that if I do not specifically indicate my preference regarding any of the forms of treatment listed above, and I do not name a surrogate to make medical treatment decisions for me, I may receive that form of treatment.

Other instructions:

I do ☐ do not ☐ want to designate another person as my surrogate to make medical treatment decisions for me if I should be incompetent and in a terminal condition, or in a state of permanent unconsciousness. I authorize my surrogate to make decisions regarding any of the medical treatments listed above as to which I do not specifically indicate my preference, and any other form of treatment not listed in this declaration.

Name and address of surrogate (if applicable): _____

_____

_____

_____

Name and address of substitute surrogate (if surrogate designated above is unable to serve): _____

_____

_____

I do ☐ do not ☐ want to make an anatomical gift of all or part of my body, subject to the following limitations, if any: _____

_____

I made this declaration on the _____ day of _____, 19___.

Declarant's signature: _____

Declarant's address: _____

_____

    If this declaration was signed by another person on behalf of and at the direction of the declarant, please explain the circumstances:

    The declarant or the person on behalf of and at the direction of the declarant knowingly and voluntarily signed this writing by signature or marked in my presence.

Witness' signature: _____

Witness' signature: _____

Witness' signature: _____

Witness' signature: _____

Please note: This declaration is based on the model form set forth in the Pennsylvania advance directive for health care act, at 20 pa. Csa 5404(b). This form may not be best suited for every individual. If you have any questions, please consult your attorney.

QUICK n̅ PAINLESS

Make photocopies of this form and make sure that your family knows where to find them now, so it won't be a problem later.

FUNERAL ARRANGEMENTS RECORD

Name: _____

Cemetery: _____ Lot #: _____

Location of cemetery deed: _____

Burial insurance: _____ Policy #: _____

Company: _____

Address: _____

_____

Phone: (   )_____ Fax: (   )_____

Have you made funeral arrangements? _____ Prepaid? _____

Funeral home: _____

Contact: _____

Address: _____

_____

Phone: (   )_____ Fax: (   )_____

Survivor's To-do List

Immediately:

- Notify friends/relatives
- (Spouse) Get documents from safety deposit box
- Make funeral arrangements
- Send obituary notices
- List all expressions of sympathy
- Arrange gathering after service
- Obtain 20 copies of death certificate
- Open checking account in your name

A COMPLETE WASTE OF TIME

The 3 Worst Things to Do When Planning for Your Future:

1. Allow yourself to think "oh, I can always do that later!"

2. Assume that your family knows "exactly how you would want things done."

3. Bury your important papers in the back-yard.

First Month:
- Establish estate bank account in deceased's name
- File for insurance benefits
- Notify insurance companies
- Notify credit card companies
- Review auto insurance policy
- Apply for pension benefits, Social Security
- Meet with attorney to begin probate
- Notify financial advisor
- Notify Keogh, IRA accounts
- Notify stockbroker

Second Month:
- Revise your will
- File estate, inheritance tax returns
- Make sure attorney files will
- Transfer real estate titles
- Transfer car titles
- Transfer insurance policies
- Change telephone utilities to your name
- Notify creditors

IF YOU'RE SO
INCLINED

Make potential credit card chaos a snap by consolidating all of your card information in one place.

CREDIT CARD INDEX

Using a simple form like this can make keeping your credit cards in order a breeze! Feel free to make more copies of this as you need to.

Credit card: _____ Account #: _____

Name(s) on card: _____ Expiration date: _____

Phone: ( )_____

If lost, call: _____

Limit: _____ Interest rate: _____

CAR INSURANCE RECORD

Company: _____

Agent's name: _____

Address: _____

Phone: (___)_____ Fax: (___)_____

E-mail: _____

Policy #: _____ Policy location: _____

Annual premium: _____ How paid: _____

Cars insured:

Make: _____ Model: _____ Year: _____

Vehicle ID #: _____ Mileage: _____

License #: _____ Owned/Leased?: _____

Name(s) of insured: _____

How many miles driven: _____

Car(s) insured:

Make: _____ Model: _____ Year: _____

Vehicle ID #: _____ Mileage: _____

License #: _____ Owned/Leased?: _____

Name(s) of insured: _____

How many miles driven: _____

YOU'LL THANK YOURSELF LATER

Use these forms to make all of the relevant information about your insurance policies available at a glance!

LIFE INSURANCE

Company name: _____

Insurance agent's name: _____ Phone: (   )_____

Address: _____

Phone: (   )_____ Fax: (   )_____

Name of insured: _____

Policy owner: _____

Policy #: _____ Policy location: _____

Whole life, variable, or term insurance? _____

Monthly premium: _____

Renewal date: _____ Dividend option: _____

Total cash value: $_____ Total death benefits: _____

Loan against policy? _____ How much? _____

Date borrowed: _____

Primary beneficiary: _____

Secondary beneficiary: _____

Congratulations! You've started down the road to realizing your financial goals, now take a break and enjoy the sunset—you deserve it!

The Lazy Way

Amount of Life Insurance Needed to Provide a Certain Monthly Income (at 3.5% Interest)

Desired Monthly Income	10 Years	15 Years	20 Years
100	10,173	14,085	17,391
200	20,346	28,170	34,782
300	30,519	42,255	52,173
400	40,692	56,340	69,564
500	50,865	70,425	86,955
1,000	101,730	140,850	173,910
2,000	203,460	281,700	347,820
3,000	305,190	422,550	521,730
5,000	508,650	704,250	869,550

LONG-TERM CARE INSURANCE

Company name: _____

Insurance agent's name: _____ Phone: (   )_____

Address: _____

Phone: (   )_____ Fax: (   )_____

Name of insured: _____

Policy owner: _____

Policy #: _____ Policy location: _____

Monthly premium: _____

Renewal date: _____

Exclusions: _____

Congratulations! You've made a molehill out of a mountain of paper-work—now sit back and read the newspaper, you've earned it!

DISABILITY INSURANCE

Company name: _____

Insurance agent's name: _____ Phone: (   )_____

Address: _____

Phone: (   )_____ Fax: (   )_____

Name of insured: _____

Policy owner: _____

Policy #: _____ Policy location: _____

Premium: _____

Renewal date: _____

Waiting period: _____ Benefit period: _____

Benefit amount: $_____

Riders/Exclusions: _____

Primary beneficiary: _____

Secondary beneficiary: _____

HEALTH INSURANCE

Company name: _____

Address: _____

Insurance agent's name: _____

Address: _____

Phone: (_____)_____ Fax: (_____)_____

Name of insured: _____

Policy owner: _____

Policy #: _____ Group #: _____

HMO, Indemnity, PPO?:_____

Premium: _____ Policy location: _____

Renewal date: _____

Riders/Exclusions: _____

REAL ESTATE

Home type: _____ Zoned? _____

Address: _____

Title in name of: _____

Deed in name of: _____

Purchase date: _____ Purchase price: _____

Current value: $_____ Assessed value: $_____

Location of deeds: _____

First mortgage held:

Mortgage type: _____ Interest: _____%

Address: _____

Phone: (   )_____ Fax: (   )_____

Monthly payment: $_____ Payment due date: _____

Amount owed: _____ Date: _____

Date due (in full): _____

Annual property insurance:

Escrow taxes? _____ Amount: _____

Line of credit: _____

Bank: _____ Account #: _____

Date opened: _____ Credit limit: $_____

Current balance: _____ Interest rate: _____%

Property tax: Amount owed: $_____ Mils: _____

Spring payment amount: $_____

Fall payment amount: $_____

QUICK ⟨ **n** ⟩ *PAINLESS*

Not only will a simple real estate form like this keep you in the know now, but should you decide to sell it will make getting all the details together absolutely effortless!

HOME EQUITY ESTIMATOR

(Use this simple worksheet to calculate the equity in your home.)

Value of your home (estimate): $_____

Subtract remaining balance of any mortgage on your home: $_____

Estimated equity: $_____

   The amount of the loan for which you qualify is based on the value of your home and your credit standing, financial status, and annual income.

A COMPLETE WASTE OF TIME

The 3 Worst Things to Do When Buying an Insurance Policy:

1. Don't shop around.

2. Assume more is better.

3. Not buy a policy that suits your needs.

MORTGAGES/LOANS

Bank: _____

Type of loan: _____ Account #:_____

Name(s) on loan: _____

Length of loan: _____

Address: _____

E-mail address: _____

Contact: _____ Work phone: (   )_____

Monthly payment: $_____ Due date: _____

Final payment: $_____ Due date: _____

Interest rate: _____% Location of loan papers: _____

IF YOU'RE SO
INCLINED

All that stock paraphernalia can get confusing! Use this simple form to keep track of your stocks!

STOCKS/BONDS TRACKING RECORDS

These series of forms will help you keep a visual record of what your stocks and bonds are really up to.

Name of Stock	Date Bought	# of Shares	Original Price	Current Shares	

FINANCIAL GOALS

Simply putting money into a savings account and figuring that someday you'll use the money for a vacation isn't specific enough. Write out your goals and plan how much you need to save each month to reach them. Use these simple worksheets to plan your ideal financial future. In each one, write down your specific savings goal. Let's say you want to take your family to "Walt Disney World," for example. Figure out the total cost of the vacation and how much you need to save each month to reach that goal. Use one of the worksheets on page 30 for each financial goal you have.

Current Price	Current Value	Date Sold	# Sold	Profit	Loss

Tracking Stock Price Per Share

Name of Stock	Date	Date	Date	Date	Date	Date	Date	Date
	$	$	$	$	$	$	$	$
	$	$	$	$	$	$	$	$
	$	$	$	$	$	$	$	$
	$	$	$	$	$	$	$	$
	$	$	$	$	$	$	$	$
	$	$	$	$	$	$	$	$
	$	$	$	$	$	$	$	$
	$	$	$	$	$	$	$	$

Mutual Fund Tracking Record

Name	Type	Date Bought	# of Shares	Price Per Share	Total Price

Bond Tracking Record

Name of Bond	Certificate #	Issue Date	Interest	Maturity Date

Current Price per Share	Dividend $	Date Sold	# of Shares Sold	# Received	Profit	Loss

One Year

Goal	Total Cost	Monthly Savings

Three Years

Goal	Total Cost	Monthly Savings

Five Years

Goal	Total Cost	Monthly Savings

Getting Time on Your Side

	The Old Way	The Lazy Way
Putting together your receipts at tax time	Weeks	2 seconds
Finding out the interest rates on your credit card	30 minutes	2 minutes
Finding out how your stocks have been performing	1 hour	5 minutes
Getting the details together when it's time to sell your home	3 weeks	1 hour
Figuring out which insurance policy is right for you	1 week	A few hours
Balancing your budget	A Saturday afternoon	30 minutes

Chapter two

Where to Go and Who to Talk to for Painless Money Management

You're not alone in the quest for organized finances, so take advantage of all the great resources available to you as you start down the road to better money management. Try these valuable sites and sources to answer your questions as you go!

INFORMATION SOURCES

General Information

Consumer Credit Counseling Service
http://www.powersource.com/cccs
Provides information about loan calculation, money management, and budgeting.

A COMPLETE WASTE OF TIME

The 3 Worst Things to Do When Putting Your Finances in Order:

1. Assume that no one else has ever had the same questions.

2. Don't get a second opinion.

3. Ignore the wealth of information at your fingertips on the Internet.

Consumer Information Catalog

Pueblo, CO 81009

719-948-4000

http://www.gsa.gov/staff/pa/cic/cic.htm

The quarterly Consumer Information Center catalog lists more than 200 helpful federal publications. Write for a free copy.

IntelliChoice

http://www.intellichoice.com

Provides dealer prices and ownership costs on many car makes and models.

Essential Information

http://www.essential.org

This site will link you to Nader-founded consumer groups including the Center for Auto Safety and the Center for Insurance Research.

Managing Your Money

http://www.ag.ohio-state.edu/~ohioline/home/money

Includes articles on "Where Does Your Money Go," "Stop Spending Leaks," "Developing a Spending Plan," and more.

National Charities Information Bureau

212-929-6300

Call to verify the legitimacy of a charity.

National Fraud Information Center

800-876-7060

Call here to report a scam or get referrals to resolve telemarketing and Internet rip-offs.

The Vault

http://www.scott-burns.com

Dallas syndicated columnist Scott Burns provides insights on personal finance subjects.

Finding an Investment Planner

American Institute of Certified Public Accountants

1211 Avenue of the Americas

New York, NY 10036

800-862-4272

American Society of CLU and ChFC

270 South Bryn Mawr Avenue

Bryn Mawr, PA 19010

800-392-6900

Lists insurance agents and planners.

Institute of Certified Financial Planners

3801 E. Florida Avenue, Suite 708

Denver, CO 80210

800-282-7526

International Association for Financial Planning

5775 Glenridge Drive NE, Suite B-300

Atlanta, GA 30328

800-945-4237

This trade group requires members to have a state license or SEC registration.

Licensed Independent Network of CPA Financial Planners

800-737-2727

Lists members who are CPSA/PFS fee-only planners in public accounting firms.

IF YOU'RE SO
INCLINED

If you're looking for help in planning your investments, make sure to check these sites for valuable information on how to find someone who is perfect for you.

If you're looking to invest your money, invest some time first by browsing on these sites to save you from headaches later on!

National Association of Personal Financial Advisors

355 West Dundee Road, Suite 197

Buffalo Grove, IL 60089

800-366-2732

Investment Information

American Savings Education Council

202-659-0670

http://www.asec.org

Commission on Saving and Investment in America

202-628-5900

Get Smart

http://www.getsmart.com

Offers information on home mortgage deals and mutual funds.

IBC Financial Data

http://www.ibcdata.com

Lists money market funds and bond funds, with data on their performance.

ICI Mutual Fund Connection

http://www.ici.org

Provides news on legislation affecting investors, sponsored by the Investment Company Institute.

Intuit

http://www.intuit.com

Offers samples of its financial management software programs, Quicken and Turbotax.

Invest-o-rama

http://www.investorama.com

Provides links to more than 2,000 investment-related sites and offers analysts' consensus reports on thousands of individual stocks, as well as tips on how to set up and run an investment club.

Motley Fool

http://www.motleyfool.com

Mutual Fund Interactive

http://www.fundsinteractive.com

Provides news and views about mutual funds.

Securities and Exchange Commission (SEC)

450 Fifth Street

Mail Stop 1-2 NW

Washington, DC 20549

http://www.sec.gov

Securities Industry Association

202-296-9410

William F. Sharpe

http://www.sharpe.stanford.edu

Sharpe, a Stanford University professor of finance, offers insights on foreign and domestic markets.

Banking

American Express Financial Advisors

800-GET-ADVICE

http://www.americanexpress.com

This handy financial site walks you through seven financial planning subjects, including the cost of procrastination.

YOU'LL THANK YOURSELF LATER

The Lazy Way is the informed way. Arm yourself with information now so you can rely upon your decision later.

QUICK ⬭ PAINLESS

Don't re-invent the wheel to keep our finances rolling, tap into these experts and see what they suggest before taking the plunge.

American Stock Exchange

800-THE-AMEX

http://www.amex.com

The Bank Rate Monitor

http://www.bankrate.com

Provides information on interest rates on everything from savings accounts to credit cards and auto loans. The monitor surveys 2,500 institutions weekly to update its figures.

Bureau of Labor Statistics

http://stats.bls.gov

This site provides an amazing amount of statistics that highlight general economic trends.

Data Broadcast Corp.

http://www.dbc.com

A site with always-updated information on the markets.

FinanCenter

http://www.financenter.com

A collection of interactive worksheets designed to help with financial decisions about homes, cars, credit cards, and more.

Financial Data Finder (Ohio State University)

http://www.cob.ohio-state.edu:80/dept/fin/overview.htm

This Web site is a good place to locate financial and economic data on the Web (and elsewhere).

Humberto Cruz

http://www.starnews.webpont.com/finance/cruz.htm

This personal finance columnist has lots to say about savings.

Internet Finance Resources

http://www.lib.lsu.edu/bus/finance.html

A Web site that constantly screens and finds new financial information on the Internet.

Invest-o-rama

http://www.investorama.com

This Web site provides plenty of financial information with links to the field of finance.

Jane Bryant Quinn column

http://www.washingtonpost.com/wp-sv/business/longterm/quinn/columns/030697.htm

A compendium of past finance columns as they appeared in the *Washington Post*, arranged by topic.

John Hancock

http://www.jhancock.com

A comprehensive site that walks you through financial subjects, taking into account financial drains like college expenses while you're trying to save.

Money Minds

800-ASK-A-CFP

Answers specific financial questions about investing over the phone ($3.95 per minute).

Morningstar, Inc.

800-735-0700

http://www.morningstar.net

Provides a wealth of mutual fund data and market news.

A COMPLETE WASTE OF TIME

The 3 Worst Things to Do When It Comes Time to Invest:

1. Assume you can do it all yourself.

2. Don't make sure that all your questions have been answered.

3. Hire a broker without checking his or her background and credentials.

NASD Regulation

http://www.nasdr.com

Find out if your broker is playing by the rules.

National Association of Investors Corp.

http://www.better-investing.org

This elaborate site includes stock evaluation help, links to Standard & Poor's company reports, and other data. Many sites give updated stock quotes and allow online trading during the day.

North American Securities Administrators

http://www.nasaa.org

If you have a problem with your broker, go here.

S&P Equity Investor Service

http://www.stockinfo.standardpoor.com

Provides news headlines and stock picks from Standard & Poor's.

Securities and Exchange Commission

http://www.sec.gov

Provides all kinds of good financial Web sites and documents.

Stock Wiz

http://www.stockwiz.com

Investment Companies

American Express Financial Advisors

http://www.americanexpress.com

Budget Master, LLC

888-44BUDGET

http://www.budgetmaster.com

Charles Schwab & Co., Inc.

800-225-8567

http://www.schwab.com

Dreyfus Service Corporation

800-THE-LION, ext. 816

http://www.dreyfus.com

The Guardian

800-662-1006

http://www.theguardian.com

INVESCO Funds Groups, Inc.

800-235-5766, ext. 104

http://www.invesco.com

Janus

800-526-8983, ext. 327

http://www.janus.com

L. Roy Papp Funds

800-421-4004

The Montgomery Funds

800-572-FUND

http://www.xperts.montgomery.com

Neuberger & Berman

800-877-9700, ext. 3404

http://www.nbfunds.com

PC Financial Network

http://www.pcfn.com

This brokerage firm provides stock quotes, research, and news from AP, UP, Reuters, BusinessWire, and Market News.

YOU'LL THANK YOURSELF LATER

You wouldn't allow your child to pick a school without researching all of the options, so make sure that you nurture your finances the same way!

Prudential Investments

800-778-6363

http://www.prudential.com

Scudder No-Load Funds

800-SCUDDER, ext. 1759

http://funds.scudder.com

Stein Roe Mutual Funds

800-338-2550

http://www.steinroe.com

Strong Funds

800-368-5597

http://www.strong-funds.com

T. Rowe Price—college

800-541-6128

http://www.troweprice.com

T. Rowe Price—rollovers

800-541-6127

http://www.troweprice.com

Transamerica Premier Funds

800-892-7587, ext. 850

http://www.transamerica.com

The Vanguard Group

800-962-5173

http://www.vanguard.com

Veritas/Ameritas Life

800-552-3553

http://www.ameritas.com/veritas

Congratulations! You've made sure that you're in the know, now sit back and sip a latte . . . you've earned it!

The Lazy Way

Internet Financial Forums

Financial Planning Forum

http://www.fponline.com

Register at this site, and then follow to the forum.

Green Jungle

http://www.greenjungle.com/pub/

Silicon Investor

http://www.techstocks.com

This discussion forum features small-cap companies.

Money Publications on the Web

Barron's

http://www.barons.com

Business Week Online

http://www.businessweek.com

The Economist

http://www.economist.com

The New York Times

http://www.nytimes.com

PR Newswire

http://www.prnewswire.com

An online money magazine with interesting commentators and an archive of business and financial press releases on company earnings and other topics, as well as links to many financial sites.

Reuters News and Quotes

http://www.reuters.com/news/

Wall Street Journal

http://www.wsj.com

QUICK **ⁿ** *PAINLESS*

Stay up to date with a click of a button, use these Web sites to track the information you need!

Credit

American Collectors Association

http://www.collector.com

Bankcard Holders of America

703-389-5445

Will send you a list of low-rate credit cards for a modest fee.

Consumer Action Good Credit

116 New Montgomery Street

San Francisco, CA 94105

800-278-6045

Consumer Credit Counseling Service

http://www.powersource.com/cccs

Learn about your rights, loan calculator, credit counseling, money management, budgeting, and general advice on consumer credit.

Equifax

(800) 685-1111

Call for a copy of your credit report.

Federal Trade Commission

http://www.ftc.gov

Here you can find out more about your rights as a consumer on a number of issues, including the Fair Credit Reporting Act.

Get Smart

http://www.getsmart.com

Offers information on credit card deals.

RAM Research Corp.

800-344-7714

Will send you a list of low-rate credit cards for a modest fee.

Trans Union

800-916-8800

Call for a copy of your credit report.

TRW (credit bureau)

800-682-7654

Call for a copy of your credit report; provides one free copy per year.

Your Use of Consumer Credit

http://idea.exnet.iastate.edu:8080/cgi/getTitleList/CREDIT

Provides dozens of resources on proper use and repair of consumer credit.

Insurance

American Society of CLU and ChFC

800-392-6900

Insurance agents and planners with an insurance orientation.

Insurance Corner

http://www.insurance-corner.com

Provides consumers some useful tips on buying auto, property, and long-term care insurance.

Insurance Information Institute

110 William Street

New York, NY 10038

212-669-9200

IF YOU'RE SO INCLINED

If you're in the market for insurance, use the Web to learn about the options out there first!

Insurance NewsNetwork

http://www.insure.com

Provides helpful hints on getting insurance, a glossary of insurance-speak, and links to information about the insurance industry. It also allows you to check on an insurance company's financial rating. Offers Life Advice pamphlets on related topics: Making a Will, Planning Your Estate, and Loss of a Loved One.

MetLife Online

800-METLIFE

http://www.lifeadvice.com

National Insurance Consumer Hotline

800-942-4242

Offers free advice about life, auto, and homeowners insurance; staffed by insurance professionals.

Taxes

Consumer Credit Counseling Service

http://www.powersource.com/cccs

Provides tax tips.

IRS by telephone

800-TAX-FORM

800-829-4477 for the Teletax line (recorded answers to common questions)

IRS online

http://www.irs.ustrea.gov

Provides a host of informational forms, all of which are available for downloading.

YOU'LL THANK YOURSELF LATER

Take a moment to browse these sites before sitting down with an agent. make sure you're speaking the same language!

Money Minds

800-ASK-A-CFP

Answers specific financial questions about taxes over the phone ($3.95 per minute).

Estate Planning

Quicken American Lawyer

800-223-6925

This software package prepares 74 legal documents such as power of attorney, a premarital agreement, and a residential real estate lease.

Willmaker and Living Trust Maker

800-992-NOLO

A software package designed for estate planning available from Nolo Press.

Real Estate

FinanCenter/Smartcalc

http://www.financenter.com

Will calculate your car and mortgage payments.

National Association of Mortgage Brokers

1735 N. Lynn Street, Suite 950

Arlington, VA 22209

Will provide a list of brokers in your area.

National Taxpayers' Union

703-683-5700

Offers a 22-page pamphlet, "How to Fight Property Taxes," for $6.95.

QUICK 🔘 *PAINLESS*

Let someone else do the hard stuff . . . try a software package designed to make managing your money a snap!

QUICK **n** PAINLESS

Use the Internet to advertise your mortgage needs; odds are someone will come to you with exactly what you're looking for!

United Homeowners Association "Mortgage Rate Shopper"

800-816-2870

On the UHA Web site you can post the type of mortgage you're looking for; mortgage brokers who monitor this page will respond if they have the loan you want.

Retirement

American Association of Retired Persons

202-434-3525

FinancCenter/Smartcalc

http://www.financenter.com

Will show you how much you need in order to retire.

Nest Egg

http://www.nestegg.com

Sponsored by Investment Dealer's Digest, this service provides news on mutual funds and stocks, and can help calculate your ideal rate of retirement saving.

Pension and Welfare Benefits Administration

U.S. Department of Labor

202-219-8776

800-998-7542 (publication hotline)

http://www.dol.gov/dol/pwba

Provides information to help prepare you for retirement.

Savings Bond Operations Office

U.S. Department of the Treasury

http://www.publicdebt.treas.gov/sav/sav.htm

Social Security Administration

800-772-1213

http://www.ssa.gov

Call for a free personal earnings and benefit estimate statement.

U.S. Department of Labor

800-998-7542

Call for a free booklet on private pensions.

Job Hunting

America's Job Bank

http://www.ajb.dni.us/cgi-biin/websrch.cgi?f_mode=f_sds

Covers employment throughout the United States.

Career Path

http://www.careerpath.com/search.html

Provides job listings in all the major daily newspapers.

Job Bank USA

http://www.jobbankusa.com/search.html

Search by key word.

Monster Board

http://www.monsterboard.com/pf/mb/client/ui/resume/build.htm

A place to build and post your own résumé.

Resumes Online

http://a2z.lycos.com/Business_and_Investing/Careers_and_Jobs Resumes_Online

A list of links to résumé posting sites.

Yahoo Employment Classifieds

http://classifieds.yahoo.com/employment.html

A COMPLETE WASTE OF TIME

The 3 Worst Things to Do When Looking for a Job:

1. Ignore the vast options out there.

2. Settle for a job that you're not comfortable with.

3. Post an out-of-date resume.

Getting Time on Your Side

	The Old Way	The Lazy Way
Getting answers to your financial questions	1 week	1 hour (on the Net!)
Learning about your investment options	1 month	A few hours
Hiring the right broker	Possibly never	30 minutes
Tracking your stocks	2 hours	5 minutes
Resolving credit debt	7 years	A few months
Understanding your insurance options	What?!	A few hours on the Net

Part 2

Simply Whip Those Finances Into Shape

Are You Too Lazy to Read About Whipping Those Finances Into Shape?

1 Organizing your life sounds good, but you like walking through piles of papers on the floor to get to your desk. If you put everything away, you might never find it again. ☐ yes ☐ no

2 Shortcuts sound good, but your life really functions better in a state of chaos. You like living in the eye of the tornado, even if life does occasionally implode. ☐ yes ☐ no

3 You know you have a CD, but you haven't a clue when it's coming due. It's the bank's job to worry about that ☐ yes ☐ no

Chapter three

Organizing Your Finances Without Agony

The best way to track your finances the lazy way is to get organized. It may take a few moments up front, but once you're organized, the job of figuring out what to do with your money is much, much easier.

TRACKING YOUR SPENDING WITHOUT TRACKING YOUR HEART RATE!

You might think life would be a lot easier if you just threw all your money in a pot and spent it mindlessly, but that's not how it works. In fact, the lazy way is the organized way. Here's how to organize your budget:

- List your income.

- List your expenses by going through your checkbook register and credit card bills for the past year.

- Categorize payments into various areas: taxes, mortgage, entertainment, insurance, clothes, and so on.

You also can track your spending by using a computer. There are a variety of computer software programs that will help you track spending and pay your bills at the same time. (For details, see Chapter 16).

You may find, however, that the truly lazy way to track spending is to simply get out a pencil and piece of paper and do it by hand—and that's okay. Sometimes a computer, like a microwave oven, seems to provide the fast way, but it really doesn't. If you're not computer literate, you first have to learn how to use the software. Then, if you track spending by computer, you've got to remember to enter the information every week or month. After a month or two, most people give up because it's a hassle to use a computer for this.

There is one benefit to computer tracking for those of you who are computer literate. If you use the most popular software package, called Quicken, to track spending and pay bills, you can get a Quicken Visa credit card. The Intellicharge feature allows you to get your monthly transactions by modem or on a disk; Quicken can then track both your credit and your check spending.

MAKING A BUDGET THAT REALLY WORKS FOR YOU

Once you've figured out where your money has been going, you can set up a plan to corral that spending.

- Looking at your past history, estimate a monthly amount for each of your spending areas: housing, insurance, clothing, and so on.

- Keep working at it until the amount going out is the same as the amount coming in.

- This is your monthly budget. Stick to it!

Congratulations! You've made a budget. Now reward yourself for taking the first step in managing your money the lazy way. Take a break and dive into a hot fudge sundae. You deserve it!

CALENDARS: DON'T FORGET, IT'S NOT JUST HOW YOU SPEND IT, BUT WHEN!

Another essential for the money manager interested in saving time is a good calendar. If you're like most folks with a job, a family, and about a million other responsibilities, you probably already have one tacked up around the house somewhere.

Now you've got to be sure to enter your financial information here, too. Enter the dates when your CDs mature—about a week before they are due. Normally, the bank should send you a notification, but if the mail gets snarled or you don't open it right away—or you

A COMPLETE WASTE OF TIME

The 3 Worst Things to Do When Setting Up a Budget:

1. Ignore your spending history.

2. Set expectations for yourself above your means.

3. Figure it will "all come in the wash."

misplace it when you do—you could miss the dates when your certificates come due.

You may want to reinvest a certificate at a different bank, or put the money in an investment that will pay more, but you can't do that if you miss the rollover date. Write it down!

You'll also want to write down due dates for your four quarterly tax payments if you're self-employed. Schedule dates several times a year to sit down with your spouse and go over your financial plan. Chances are, if you record a date on your calendar you're more likely to keep the appointment.

ORGANIZING YOUR LIFE: MAKING A PERSONAL FINANCIAL SYSTEM

We've given you lots of worksheets, tear-out forms, and so on, but without a system, they are just a bunch of papers that will probably get lost.

Remember, the lazy way is the organized way. So sit down at your computer and make this list of all your important personal finance information:

- Bank accounts (and your personal banker), with numbers and addresses

- Where to find your safe deposit box and keys

- Location of your will, and the attorney who drew it up

- Executor of your will

- Accountant's name, address, and phone number

- Investment advisors'/brokers' names, addresses, and phone numbers

- Location of trust documents

- Your insurance policies and insurance agents

- Employee benefits and the phone number of the office that handles them

- All debts and money owed to you

- Social Security numbers of all family members

- Location of all properties, and where the deeds are

- Location of tax records

- Location of securities and retirement accounts

- Credit card account numbers, addresses, and phone numbers

Safety Deposit Box: Protecting the Important Things

Now that you've made your list, make sure to get some type of fireproof home safe or safety deposit box. In it should go your family's birth certificates and marriage certificates; death certificates of close family members; all documents relating to separation, divorce, and child custody; military service records; citizenship or adoption papers; licenses; passports; permits; Social Security cards; and family health records (including records of vaccinations and surgeries, and lists of all health care providers).

Household Inventory: Keeping Track of What You Have

Everyone should have a household inventory, but writing down lists of everything you have and supplementing that with photographs is an incredibly time-consuming practice. Who's got time for all that?

Instead, simply videotape every room in your house. Take pictures of every room, every closet, and every open drawer. Make sure to include jewelry.

If you don't own a video camera, borrow one from a friend or rent one for a day. When the tape is finished, file it in your safety deposit box. If your house is ever damaged or destroyed, you'll have a record of everything you own for the insurance company.

Credit Card Statements: Keep a Close Eye on These!

Check every statement as soon as it comes in to make sure that every charge on it is really yours. It's not hard—especially with online credit card use—for a thief to get hold of your number to buy things and charge them to your account.

Should you save your old credit card receipts? Some people squirrel them all away, but after 1991, when you could no longer deduct the interest, this became less important.

Bills and Receipts: Which Ones Should I Keep and Where Do I Put Them?

You should keep medical and drug bills for at least a year. When tax time rolls around, you can deduct any medical

If you're a gold card member, your card may send you an "end of the year" summary statement with everything you've charged neatly categorized. This is a great way to organize things for taxes. When your taxes are done, simply file this organizer with your receipts.

bill not covered by insurance that exceeds 7½ percent of your adjusted gross income. If you tally everything up and you aren't entitled to a deduction, throw the bills away.

Every expense that is tax deductible should be documented by a receipt. This sounds like a hassle, but it isn't. Just designate one big drawer as your "receipt" drawer and throw all your potential tax deductions in there. If you've got time, you can file them neatly in some type of household management book. But for the rest of us who just don't have the time, chucking them in the drawer is fine. It takes only about an hour to go through all of the receipts when tax time rolls around, and if they're all in one place it's a cinch! Be sure to keep any receipts for home improvement expenses in that tax drawer.

The IRS really likes it if the receipt is clipped to the related check, so you might want to throw your canceled checks in the drawer, too.

Make it a habit to keep receipts for gifts you've bought, too, until you know for sure that Aunt Agatha really did want those ruby red slippers. It's especially important if you paid in cash.

ELECTRONIC ORGANIZERS: POCKET-SIZED PERSONAL ASSISTANTS

If you're a harried, hassled, and hurried money manager, you should take comfort in the fact that you're living in the best possible century, because modern technology has come up with some really great solutions for your lifestyle.

YOU'LL THANK YOURSELF LATER

Keep receipts for big-ticket items—furs, silver, and so on—in a safety deposit box or fireproof home safe. You'll need them to prove a claim in the event of a fire or theft, in case the insurance company gets grumpy and wants to see proof.

There are a wide range of electronic gadgets and products out there just waiting to make your financial life easier. Constantly forgetting appointments with your financial advisors? Forget when that CD is coming due? Electronic calendars come in a variety of styles, sizes, and prices, and many have beepers to alert you to special appointments.

Other electronic devices combine address books, calendars, spreadsheets, budget worksheets, and other business software, and can be connected to your computer for downloading important economic information. You can also tap into your online files and e-mail—all this, and the gadget fits into your pocket, too!

Ever been driving down the road and suddenly remembered you have to call your broker to make an important transaction? A credit-card-sized electronic memo device can make notes for you. Just press a button, record your brief reminder, and keep on driving.

There are also a number of free "reminder" services available on the Internet that can be set up to alert you to upcoming important engagements, appointments, and so on. When the day approaches, you'll get a "reminder" e-mail, and another one will arrive a day or so before the important date.

A COMPLETE WASTE OF TIME

The 3 Worst Things to Do When Organizing Your Life:

1. Not bother to make a budget.

2. Forget to save your tax-deductible receipts.

3. Get a safety deposit box, but forget to tell anyone where the key is or what bank the box is in.

Getting Time on Your Side

	The Old Way	The Lazy Way
Reminding yourself of an appointment	5 minutes	4 seconds
Recording a date on the calendar	5 minutes	3 seconds
Taking household inventory	45 minutes	20 minutes
Putting together receipts at tax time	Days	Moments
Tracking your spending	Hours	10 minutes
Figuring out your net worth	Weeks	A few hours (tops!)

Chapter four

Shortcuts for Big Savings

There are a host of quick things you can do to save money the easy way. They don't take a lot of brain power or time. Skim this list and see if you can incorporate some of these hints today!

SAVING AND BANKING QUICK TIPS

A few minutes now can save you hours later! Plus, each of these tips will help you save some extra money at the same time!

- Each day, take a one-dollar bill out of your wallet and put in into a bank deposit envelope. At the end of a month, deposit the money into your savings account.

- Arrange for regular monthly bills (like your insurance premiums) to be paid automatically from your bank account. It's usually free, and you save yourself time, hassle, and the cost of the check and the stamp for the bill.

Cut down on ATM withdrawals. Visit the cash machine for spending money just once a week, and make that money last for seven days. Make sure you stick to your own bank's ATM—different ATMs will charge fees.

Throw all of your coins in a jar. Once a month, count the change and deposit it in your account.

Don't put that IRS refund or other rainy-day savings into a money market deposit account or a passbook savings account. You'll only get about 2.5 percent interest, which can be beaten just about anywhere. A no-load money market mutual fund is the place for "emergency" money.

Go over your budget and see if you can trim a bit off any category. If you do, deposit this money in a savings account.

Call Money Minds (800-ASK-A-CFP) for answers to specific questions about investing or tax preparation. The cost: $3.95 per minute. This independent group of CPAs and certified financial planners also offers more in-depth analysis, charging an hourly rate.

Put all your loose change in a piggy bank. You'll feel too guilty to raid the bank once it's in there. When it's full, tote it to the bank and deposit the money.

Consider refinancing your mortgage if your interest rate drops by one percentage point.

- Your bank may lower or drop checking fees if your paycheck is deposited directly into your account by your employer. Plus it saves time!

GETTING AND KEEPING YOUR CREDIT IN GOOD SHAPE

We love having those credit cards when we're in an emergency, but we hate them when the bills come. Here are some tips to cut the "hate" out of our "love-hate" relationship with credit!

- If you're having trouble paying off a large balance on your credit card, switch to a card with a low rate. For an easy way to find a card like this, call Bankcard Holders of America (703-389-5445) or RAM Research Corp. (800-344-7714) for a list.

- Don't shop for a bargain and then put it on your credit card unless you can pay off the balance at the end of the month. In the end, you'll pay more in interest than you saved.

- Cut down on your credit card fees (which can mount up to more than $100 a year) by axing all but one or two cards.

- Negotiate a lower interest rate on your credit card balance. Call the 800 number listed on your card, ask for the supervisor, and say that you've had lots of offers to transfer your balance. Ask, "Can you do something for me?"

IF YOU'RE SO INCLINED

Spend some time now to lower your credit card interest rates and save both time and money later on!

YOU'LL THANK YOURSELF LATER

Remember the children's fable about the Ant and the Grasshopper? Be an Ant! Stock up now on things you'll need later!

HASSLE-FREE SHOPPING

If you want to shop the lazy way, look no farther than your computer. Whether you're seeking deals on books, music, or even your next car, Cyberspace is the place to go.

- The best thing about online shopping is the ability you have to comparison shop. If you're looking for a new CD player, you could go driving around to five or six stereo places. Instead, you can simply visit a site like CompareNet, enter your price range, and shop from home.

- If it's books you're looking for, Amazon.com and BarnesandNoble.com are two sites you don't want to miss. You can choose from millions of titles, or enter an author or title and let the service do your browsing. Because virtual sites don't have to maintain the traditional overhead of salesclerks, rent, and shelf space, they can pass on significant savings of up to 30 or 40 percent.

- Got a favorite author whose books you always snap up? With Amazon.com, you can enter the author's name and your e-mail address and be notified online whenever that author's next book is published.

- Shop the "wrong" season: At the end of summer, buy summer stuff for the next year; at the end of winter, do the same thing.

- The day after Christmas, stock up on Christmas cards, wrapping paper, and bows.

- Shop mail order catalogs to save time: You don't have to drive around and fight crowds at the mall. If you get lots of catalogs, you can often comparison shop and find the same item much cheaper in one catalog over another.

- On the other hand, don't shop catalogs just to save sales tax—you'll usually pay more in shipping costs. To cut down on these costs, shop from catalogs with a set amount for one order, and then combine your order with those of friends.

- If you're mailing gifts, save time and money by ordering from a mail order catalog and having the gift wrapped and sent directly to the recipient.

- The day after Halloween, shop for discount costumes. You can buy your son's Darth Vader costume for next year, and have that much more time and money to stock up on great candy for the neighborhood kids!

- Start looking at these sites to get the most for your money online:

Excite's Shopping Channel	http://www.excite.com
FirstAuction	http://www.Firstauction.com
Amazon	http://www.Amazon.com
Barnes and Noble	http://www.BarnesandNoble.com
CompareNet	http://www.compare.net.com

Congratulations! It's only November 1st, but you're already prepared for next Halloween. Take a break with your kids! You've earned it!

The Lazy Way

QUICK ⬤ PAINLESS

Before you touch that thermostat, reach for a sweater. You'll feel that much cozier and your bill will stay down.

HOW TO CHANGE THE HOUSE WITHOUT KILLING THE BANK ACCOUNT

Want a new look for your house without creating a big hole in your wallet? Try these tips!

- Don't wallpaper the bathroom: Buy a new shower curtain or bath mat.

- Frame a poster; change artwork regularly.

- Moving? Do it before the most popular months: June, July, and August. Opt for a weekday, when movers are less busy. If your move is job-related, expenses may be deductible. Save receipts and consult IRS publication #521: "Moving Expenses" (call 800-829-3676 for the form).

- Switch to washable fabrics and save about $200 a year in dry cleaning bills (even considering the cost of washing and drying at home).

- Cut out just one premium cable channel a year and save about $95 a year.

- Lower the thermostat; each degree cuts the heating bill by 3 percent. In the summer, save on air conditioning by raising the thermostat.

FINANCIAL FINE TUNING: INSURANCE AND MORTGAGES

Feel as if your mortgage and insurance will never be under control? Use these tips to show those pesky payments who's boss (and make sure that you're not paying too much while you're at it!)

- Contact the National Insurance Consumer Hotline (800-942-4242) for free advice about life, auto, and homeowners' insurance. Sponsored by insurance industry trade associations, the hotline is staffed with insurance pros who tell you what to do if you're having trouble filing a claim, or how to buy insurance if you need it.

- To find out how much you'll save on your mortgage with extra payments, check out the "calculator" portion of the Web site for Better Homes and Gardens Family Money magazine (http://www.familymoney. com).

- If you and your spouse have one income and two children, you should have five times your annual income in life insurance. More kids means more insurance; fewer kids or more income means less insurance. There's not one formula for everyone.

- Raise your deductible on collision and comprehensive coverages, or if you have an older car, drop collision insurance altogether. These simple steps—just a phone call away—can save hundreds of dollars a year.

A COMPLETE WASTE OF TIME

The 3 Worst Things to Do When It Comes to Insurance and Mortgages:

1. Undervalue the benefits to increasing the number of payments you make over time.

2. Assume that any insurance policy is right for you.

3. Get the wrong coverage for your car.

"Brown-bagging" it not only saves you time to enjoy your lunch break (no more standing in line at the deli!), but it also saves plenty of cash too . . . check it out!

HOW TO AVOID EATING YOUR WALLET WITHOUT A DIET!

Love food but hate the grocery bills you keep racking up? Try these tips for smarter shopping!

- Prepare a list and stick to it. Ignore the end-of-aisle displays. Shop as quickly as you can, for every minute you're in the store, you spend an average of $1.70.

- Freeze odd bits of leftover meat, vegetables, or uncooked fresh pasta. When you're strapped for time later on, you can throw them in a pot for soup, or add them to eggs for an omelet.

- Buy food in its original form (you'll save money).

- Stop serving big pieces of meat at every meal. Eat more rice and pasta. It's easier to cook, anyway.

- The least expensive cereals are puffed wheat or rice, store-brand corn flakes, and store-brand oat circles. It's just as easy to reach for these as for premium brands.

- Throw together leftover meat, vegetables, and noodles to make a big pot of soup. It's faster and cheaper than making individual sandwiches.

- Freeze odd bits of cheese and use later for tacos, omelets, and so on.

- Carrying a brown-bag lunch just two days a week instead of spending $5 each day on a meal will save you about $300 a year. It's fast, it's easy, and it saves money; packing a lunch five days a week will save about $750 a year.

- Buy meat on loss-leader sales (advertised on the front and back pages of the store's weekly flyer). These are items that the store takes a loss on, hoping to lure you into buying more expensive items as well.

VACATION WITHOUT BREAKING YOUR BACK, OR THE BANK!

Need a vacation but don't want to have to pull three weeks of overtime so that you can afford it? Try these alternatives out to make the most of your vacation without working yourself to the bone just to get on the plane!

- For the easiest, fastest way to get the best hotel rates (up to 65 percent off), check out a booking service: Quikbook (800-789-9887), at http://www.quikbook.com; Accommodation Express (800-444-7666), at http://www.accommodationexpress.com; Hotel Reservation Network (800-964-6835), at http://www.80096hotel.com.

- Look into renting a college dorm room for your vacation—it costs as little as $12 for singles, $20 for doubles. Check out "Campus Lodging Guide" at your library or call 800-525-6633 for more information.

- Consider a house swap. Exchange your home with somebody who lives in an area where you'd like to vacation. Contact Vacation Exchange Club at 800-638-3841, Intervac U.S. at 800-756-HOME, or Trading

YOU'LL THANK YOURSELF LATER

Make sure you ask for value plans or lower rates where available— they may not be advertised!

Congratulations! You're finally going on a vacation you can enjoy! Now take a few moments to daydream about the relaxation you've worked so hard for!

Homes International at 800-877-8723. What could be easier?

- Book your own accommodations. The reservation desk doesn't usually quote you a cheaper rate unless you ask. Ask, "What's the best you can do for me?"

- Find cheaper airline seats by surfing the Internet. A variety of specialty travel sites can regularly send you notice of the cheapest seats to destinations that you preselect. If you have the flexibility of last-minute travel, you can save big.

- Cruise during the less expensive season (mid-August to mid-December).

- Let your travel agent know if you're flexible about dates. You might be able to save big by traveling a week earlier or later.

- Travel on a Saturday when possible, and buy the ticket in advance; you often can save big on airfare.

- When booking a cruise, ask for a run-of-the-ship rate. You pay a minimum rate and you may be able to upgrade a week before you leave.

- Travel off season—it will be more relaxing, and you'll pay less.

- Cash in on fare wars. If the ticket price drops after you've bought your ticket, you may be able to trade it in for a cheaper seat.

- Take advantage of frequent flyer miles; the more you fly, the more points you earn. Some credit cards also offer frequent flyer miles.

- Call a hotel consolidator for great rates in certain city hotels at no charge. Call Hotel Reservations Network at 800-96-HOTELS or Quikbook at 800-789-9887.

- When booking a cruise, choose an interior room on a lower deck; new ships have standard rooms throughout.

- Call more than one car rental company, and ask for weekly rates if you need to rent for at least five days. Smaller local companies may be able to beat the prices of the big guys.

- Stay over a weekend. You'll usually find much cheaper hotel rates if you stay Saturday night. When you call, find out if there's a weekend package. In Washington, DC, for example, the Grand Hyatt slashes its midweek rate of $265 per night to just $119 for the weekend.

- When traveling on the road, consider buying sandwiches and a snack at a local market or deli and eating al fresco instead of in an expensive restaurant. It's a lot less stressful and much cheaper.

- Always fill the gas tank in your rental car before dropping it off to avoid drop-off fees.

QUICK 🔲 *PAINLESS*

More expensive is not necessarily better—use what gas is right for your car. No doubt you'll save money in the process.

CARS AND CASH: HOW TO DRIVE FOR LESS

You need your car to get to work, and you need your paycheck to keep the car running so you can get to work. Does this sound familiar? Start incorporating some of these ideas to keep those car cents down to a dull roar!

- Start using regular gas unless your owner's manual specifies premium. If regular is 20 cents below premium, you'll save about $85 a year per car.

- Carpool and save on tolls, gas, and parking. In medium-large cities, carpoolers can save about $1,500 a year.

- Try buying tires through mail order and save. Vendors can ship the tires directly to your garage if you wish. Try Tire Rack, (800) 428-8355.

- When renting, decline the extra insurance if your own insurance will cover you.

- Next time you get new tires, buy radials. They produce less friction and drag, and cut fuel consumption by up to 10 percent.

- Buying a car? Try one of the online car-buying services. They can alert you to the best price around, without your having to lift a telephone.

- You can save hundreds of dollars by pumping gas yourself. Choose a station that lets you zip your credit card right there at the pump; then you don't have to waste time and energy running into the store to pay.

A COMPLETE WASTE OF TIME

The 3 Worst Things to Do When It Comes to Your Car:

1. Pay more for something you don't really need.

2. "Forget" to keep up on car maintenance.

3. Pay for rental car insurance when you're already covered by your own policy.

REVAMP YOUR MONEY ROUTINES IN SMALL WAYS

Ever notice at the end of the day that we seem to spend a lot of money on absolutely nothing? Keep an eye on those little things that make up each day, and see what you are spending that money on!

- Rethink your routine purchases; a cup of coffee every day at work can easily add up to more than $150 a year.

- Want to give a helping hand to young people starting out on their own? Try this "financial starter package": computer software for budgeting, writing checks, and paying bills; an accordion file for keeping financial records; and a subscription to *Kiplinger's Personal Finance Magazine* (one of the best personal finance teaching tools).

- Don't carry too much cash. If you withdraw $100 from the cash machine every few days, you'll be amazed how quickly it disappears. You'll be less likely to make impulse buys if you write a check.

- Stop eating in restaurants so often; brown bag it instead.

- Pay down your credit cards. A balance of $1,000 means you're wasting $200 a year on interest.

GIFTS THAT DON'T TAKE SO MUCH

Love to give gifts, but hate that empty wallet feeling? Balance your desire to give with your need to save. Try these out!

- A terrific gift for newlyweds or new parents: two hours of counseling with a fee-only financial planner. They'll learn about budgeting, saving, insurance, investing, and other money tips. Fee-only planners charge only for their time, and won't be trying to sell any products.

- The day after Halloween, look for great bargains on "fairy princess" or "bride" dresses, to give as Christmas or Hanukkah gifts for little girls' fancy dress-up clothes.

- Limit gift spending to a sum that can be paid off in three months if you have to charge some of your gifts.

YOU'LL THANK YOURSELF LATER

Give from the heart, not the wallet. Don't let the "giving season" give you a pile of credit card debt.

Getting Time on Your Side

	The Old Way	The Lazy Way
Tracking your ATM Withdrawals	3 hours	5 minutes
Preparing for Halloween	2 weeks	A few hours
Buying a car Insurance policy	3 hours	1 hour
Getting control of your credit card interest rates	Never!	1 quick phone call
Paying off your mortgage	15 years	Half the time!
Taking your lunch break	30 minutes	1 hour

Chapter
five

Modest Monthly Management

It's not good enough to set up a financial plan; you've got to follow through with your ideas as well. We've assembled a year's worth of follow-up tips, beginning with things you need to do right this moment and followed, month by month, with what you should be doing to keep up with your finances.

Grab a cup of coffee, sit back, and start reading.

DO THIS NOW

▪ Grant power of attorney to someone you trust. Choose someone besides your spouse; if you both are injured or incapacitated, you'll need someone to be able to deposit checks, pay bills, and handle other financial matters for you.

▪ Make an "important person" list with the names and phone numbers of people to contact in an emergency. Include your lawyer, accountant, insurance agent, broker, and others. Give a copy to a friend or family member.

- Make an inventory of your safety deposit box. Keep copies at home, and let relatives know where the copies are.

- Make sure you and your spouse have up-to-date wills. Make sure you name guardians for children under age 18.

- Grab your video camera and record everything you own, every room and every drawer. File the finished tape in your safety deposit box.

January

- Make an appointment with your tax advisor. If you start working before the March–April busy season, you'll have more time to figure out how to reduce your tax bill.

- Pay your fourth quarterly estimated tax payment.

- Make a semiannual review of your financial plan: Call your advisor and decide which stocks, bonds, and mutual funds to sell. Consider selling slow growers that you've held for 18 months or more, in order to benefit from the new long-term capital gains tax rates.

February

- Fill out your tax return as soon as possible if you're going to be applying for financial aid for your college-age student. Schools require current tax

QUICK 🔲 PAINLESS

Use a video camera to record your home inventory in a few hours instead of spending weeks with a pen and paper!

information before considering awards. Aid forms should be filed now.

- Put all your 1099 and W-2 forms in a drawer along with all the receipts you've been saving. Keeping your tax information in one place will be a help when you begin assembling the information for taxes.

- Start buying generic drugs by mail and save. Try Medi-Mail, 800-922-3444; AARP Pharmacy Service, 800-456-2277; or DPD Action Pharmacy, 800-452-1976.

QUICK **n** PAINLESS

Start planning for next year now, and keep yourself ahead of the game!

March

- Draw up a planned budget for next year. Tracking expenses is the best way to find extra cash for investing.

- Buy an EE U.S. Savings Bond—the safest investment around—for as little as $50. There's no fee and no state or local income tax. If used to pay for college, federal income tax is waived under certain circumstances.

April

- Pay your first quarterly estimated tax payment.

- As you begin your spring cleaning, update your insurance coverage. Take photos or a video of all

your possessions, and store the pictures (or the tape) in your safety deposit box.

- Refile your withholding tax (form W-4) with your employer; take all possible exemptions and deductions. You want to pay your exact tax in 1999, and not get a refund, so that you can invest the extra income yourself and earn interest.

May

- Shop sales for winter clothing, sports equipment, and blankets.

- Get ready for your vacation: Call your insurance agent to find out details about health insurance when traveling outside the United States.

- For additional coverage, try TravMed at 800-732-5309 or U.S. Assist at 800-756-5900.

June

- Pay your second quarterly estimated tax payment.

- Make a semiannual review of your financial plan: Call your advisor and decide which stocks, bonds, and mutual funds to sell. Consider selling slow growers that you've held for 18 months or more, in order to benefit from the new long-term capital gains tax rates.

July

- Clear out your closets and hold a yard sale. Donate whatever doesn't sell to charity; get a letter of value from the charity for tax purposes.

- Call your public utility. If you've had an account for more than a year, ask for your deposit back. Then invest the amount.

August

- Challenge your property tax bill. Most states allow owners to challenge these bills within two to four months after they are mailed. Read the National Taxpayers' Union's 22-page pamphlet, "How to Fight Property Taxes" (703-683-5700).

- Shop for deals on barbecue grills, bathing suits, and other summer goods.

- Save for holiday gifts instead of charging, but don't put the money into a no-interest "Christmas Club." Instead, open a separate savings account or money market account.

September

- Review your employee benefits; October and November typically are the benefit sign-up period at many companies.

IF YOU'RE SO
INCLINED

Tired of opening chock full closets with items you can't remember buying? Hold a yard sale and gain some money back, as well as some much needed storage space!

- Have your kids figure out how much they earned during vacation. Dependent kids must file a tax return if they earned more than $4,150 a year. Get publication #4 (Student's Guide to Federal Income Tax) or call 800-829-3676 for more information.
- Pay the third installment of estimated quarterly income tax.

October

- Organize financial documents before December 31. Consider selling stocks, bonds, or mutual funds that have declined in value.
- Buy an air conditioner now and save big—anywhere from $50 to $200. When the weather is hot, prices go up.
- Double up on mortgage payments. Instead of a $1,000 monthly mortgage, pay $500 twice a month; you'll pay off a 30-year loan in 22 years.

November

- Stop by your employee benefits office. If you can, consider signing up for long-term disability or a 401(k) plan. Compare health plans for the best deal.
- Lower your thermostat by one or two degrees. You'll be surprised how much you save.

YOU'LL THANK YOURSELF LATER

Pay your tax quarterlies early and stop paying those late fees!

December

- Buy a car. Dealers are under pressure to clear out showrooms to make way for next year's models. To check out car deals, visit this Web site: http://www.intellichoice.com.

- If you're self-employed, open a Keogh account by December 31. You have until April 15 to fund it with up to $30,000 (or 25 percent of adjusted self-employment earnings—whichever is less). Keogh earnings are tax deferred.

- Shop for wrapping paper, ribbons, and holiday cards immediately after the holidays.

Congratulations! You've stayed on top all year, now sleep in a little bit—you deserve the rest!

The Lazy Way

Getting Time on Your Side

	The Old Way	The Lazy Way
Creating a home inventory	Weeks	A few hours
Getting ready for the year ahead	365 days	A few hours
Paying your taxes 4 times a year	3 weeks	5 minutes
Sorting through all the stuff you don't use to find the one thing you need	Days	Don't! You have a yard sale!
Paying late fees	30 minutes	Never again!
Tracking investments	1 hour per month	5 minutes each week

Part 3

Quick and Easy Ways to Get all of Your Money Matters in Order

Are You Too Lazy to Read the Chapters on Getting Your Money Matters in Order?

1 You don't see the point in giving your daughter an allowance if she just blows it on bubble gum, Barbies, and blue lipstick. ☐ yes ☐ no

2 You don't have enough money left over at the end of the week to buy a box of Chiclets, so forget about even considering investing. ☐ yes ☐ no

3 You don't need a real estate agent because she'd probably just mention that buried toxic waste dump in the backyard anyway. ☐ yes ☐ no

Breathe Easy Basic Banking

You're late to work, the gas gauge is hovering on "E"—and you're out of cash. But wait! There's a cash machine up ahead. You pull in, take $20 out of the machine, and shove the ATM slip into your console along with the other 35 slips you haven't had a chance to file. As you take off, a cloud of slips sift gently to the floor, where you know they will disappear in another day or so.

This could be one reason why your accounts never balance, why you've been bouncing checks from here to Sheboygen, why the very thought of banking brings a knot to your throat. But don't worry—there is a painless way to handle your everyday banking chores. With today's banks eager for your business, they keep coming up with easier, quicker shortcuts to handle your money than you ever thought possible.

The first chore when it comes to banking is finding an institution that fits your lifestyle. When picking a bank, look

for a small community corporation that caters to the lazy money manager. You'll know you've hit pay dirt if they offer things like telephone banking, online services, drive-up windows late on Fridays and early on Saturdays, and so on. You live in the big city and there are no small banks? Look for a small branch of a big bank.

Smaller banks are a smart choice because they:

- charge less for loans
- pay more on savings
- set lower deposit minimums
- allow you to know the staff (which helps at loan time)

SAVE YOURSELF FROM THOSE BANK FEES!

Banks are not always as buttoned-up as you might think. You *can* save on banking fees, especially if you're a customer the bank would like to attract. If you have enough money in the bank, you may be able to obtain fee discounts, fee waivers, and/or interest discounts because the bank regards you as a valuable client. The fee waiver can save you ATM fees, check fees, travelers check fees, and so on.

Most folks don't realize this is possible. Talk with your banker and find out how much money you need to put in a checking or savings account to save on fees.

If you hate paying fees to use a different ATM machine:

- Plan ahead: Get cash at your bank for the weekend when you deposit your paycheck on Friday.

- Use the machine at a convenience store to access cash (most don't charge fees).

- Use your ATM as a debit card to pay for items; don't use it to get cash at a "foreign" machine.

WHICH ACCOUNT WILL WORK FOR YOU?

Okay, now you've located your bank—but who's got time to read about all the different kinds of accounts they're offering with the free toaster this week? Here's the least you need to know. Read it once and you may never need to read it again.

1. Choose the checking account with *no* interest. Most interest-bearing checking accounts offer about 1.35 percent interest, but you usually need to maintain a balance of between $1,000 and $5,000 to earn it. If you don't—and let's face it, most of us don't have the time to worry about whether we do or not— you'll pay a fee that often tops seven dollars a month. If your balance dips below the minimum just a few times (hey, none of us are perfect!), you've canceled out all the interest you could earn for the year.

2. If you don't write many checks a month, choose no-frills accounts. If you write only a couple of checks each month, go for the checking account that has

QUICK nn PAINLESS

Use our list of useful banking tips now and make choosing an account later a breeze!

low (or no) fees and offers the first 10 or 15 checks for free.

3. If you write lots of checks, avoid a money market account. You can write checks with this type of interest-bearing account, and you'll earn more interest than with checking or savings accounts. But you have to maintain a higher minimum balance to start earning interest. You can make only six transfers per month, whether to another account or to other people, but remember, only three of these can be by check.

SAVING MONEY THE LAZY WAY

Now that we've got checking accounts out of the way, we can move on to the really good stuff: saving. There are as many reasons why people don't save money as there are things to save up for.

The problem with those of us who don't have time to fuss with details is that we also tend to have an "all or nothing" attitude: If I can't save $100 a week, why bother to save anything? So you blow your bonus on a sweater at Neiman Marcus, and then you wonder why you're further in the hole than ever.

There's no place for this attitude when it comes to managing your money. Saving anything is better than saving nothing. That means if all you can spare is 10 cents a week, then stick that dime in your piggy bank and start dreaming.

Really. It's that simple.

IF YOU'RE SO INCLINED

If you want to close out your account, find out when your bank credits the interest first, because you're likely to lose money if you close it out before the interest gets compounded.

It's just not true that you need a lot of money in order to invest. The idea that only the rich can invest was probably started by the same folks who insisted women were too addle-brained to vote.

Not convinced? Here's a reality check: If you invest just $50 a month at 8 percent interest, in 25 years you'll triple your money. The sooner you start, the more you make.

All you have to do is start from where you are right now. So you say you don't know a commodity option from a calliope? Doesn't matter. You don't have to have an MBA from Harvard to start saving. You don't have to know what pork bellies are and whether they have a future.

What you do have to do is decide to start from where you are. Reach into your pocket. Grab the handful of change. Put it in a piggy bank, a Band-Aid box, or an envelope, but put it somewhere and then drop it in the bank when you get a chance.

There. You've begun. In a minute, we'll talk about some quick ways to figure out what sort of account to drop it in once you get to the bank. And from there, it's only a short hop from saving to investing. Once you realize how important it is, you can usually find the money.

In fact, there are a range of painless ways to find money:

- Pay off the balance on your credit cards. Once that's done, try saving the amount equal to the interest you were paying each month.

A COMPLETE WASTE OF TIME

The 3 Worst Things to Do When Saving Money:

1. Throw away your pocket change.

2. Spend cash gifts or windfalls.

3. Wait until later to start saving money.

- The next time you get an unexpected windfall, invest it instead of spending it.

- Got your heart set on an expensive new suit? Don't buy it if you planned on putting it on your credit card. Instead, save that amount of money.

You'll be surprised how quickly your money builds up. Let's say you spend $1.80 a day on a donut and coffee at work. If you took that $1.80 a day, five days a week, for 10 years, and dropped that in a piggy bank, you'd have $4,300 in 10 years. If you invested it at 12 percent interest, you would have $8,300—all by saving up that $1.80 a day. It's the lazy way to save. After all, if you keep on buying that donut and coffee every day, in 10 years you won't have anything to show for it except an extra 10 pounds.

IN SEARCH OF HASSLE-FREE SAVINGS ACCOUNTS

Your bank will probably offer you a choice of savings accounts. The two most popular are passbook savings and statement savings. Passbook savings accounts are a type that provides you with a record book in which your deposits and withdrawals are entered so you can keep track of your account. This record book must be presented when you make deposits and withdrawals. With a statement savings account, your bank simply mails you a monthly statement that shows withdrawals and deposits for the account. The account that offers the least hassle is probably the statement savings, since you don't need to remember to bring the little book along whenever

QUICK ⬭ PAINLESS

To find a spare $25 a month to invest, don't cut out a whole budget category. Just take a bit from different areas—two dollars from "gifts," a dollar from "clothes," three dollars from "vacation."

you want to make a deposit or withdrawal. It's also easier to keep tracking of accruing interest.

CERTIFICATES OF DEPOSIT: GAIN INTEREST WITHOUT THE HEADACHE

While saving in a straight savings account is better than hiding it under the bed, it's not much better. The reason: inflation. Keeping your funds in savings accounts means that your money is actually worth less in future years because inflation has eaten away at its purchasing ability. Cash in your pocket, in a regular checking account, or in most savings accounts is nice to have (it's better than frittering it away), but it doesn't grow. The clearest example of inflation is seen by looking at the price of a first-class stamp. What cost five cents to mail in 1965 now costs 32 cents in 1998.

If you have some money squirreled away in your sofa cushions because you've never gotten around to doing something with it, listen up. An easy way to earn more interest than you'd get in a regular bank account is to put that money in a certificate of deposit (CD). CDs earn more interest than a savings account, and they're a good solution if you don't have time to worry over the stock market. Once the money is stashed in a CD, you don't have to worry about what the Japanese yen is doing or whether the market has gone bear or bull—your interest is accruing right on schedule.

With CDs, what you buy is what you get. If you choose a six-month CD at 5 percent interest, that's what you'll have when you cash in the certificate six months

A COMPLETE WASTE OF TIME

The 3 Worst Things to Do with Your Investments:

1. **Put all your money in one account.**

2. **Invest in things you don't have a clue about.**

3. **Put money you can't afford to lose in something risky.**

If you have $2,000 to invest that you might need before the CD matures, buy more than one CD. Split the money up among several smaller-value CDs. Or stagger them so they don't all come due at the same time.

from now. No muss, no fuss. CDs mature anywhere from three months to 10 years—and the longer the term, the more money you'll earn in interest. If you have to withdraw the money before the term is up, you'll pay a penalty of up to six months' interest.

If you're the sort of person who's too busy to remember to see the dentist twice a year, you may have trouble keeping track of when your CD due dates are approaching—but never fear. Your bank will send you a friendly reminder when your CDs are almost ready to mature. Most will renew automatically, so if you don't notify the bank that you want your money at maturity, the bank will just roll over your CD for another term. When they do this, of course, you'll get whatever the current interest rate is, not what you had before.

BUT WAIT! LOOK AT WHAT A MONEY MARKET CAN DO!

If you've scraped at least $1,000 out of those sofa cushions but don't want to tie it up for several months at a time, you qualify for a money market deposit account. Money markets aren't for those who write lots of checks, since you're limited to six monthly withdrawals, but they pay a variable interest rate (usually more than you'd get in a regular savings account). Unlike a CD, you can withdraw the money any time, up to three checks a month with three automatic withdrawals (to pay for things like your mortgage). You'll pay a fee if your deposit falls below the minimum, so you should use this only if you use your checking account for regular business and you're just looking to stash some money as an emergency buffer. Wherever you open the money market fund, make sure the interest is more than what you could earn on a savings account.

BANKING IN THE 21ST CENTURY

The most exciting thing to hit the banking world for busy, harried folks has been the advent of the telecommunications industry. If you've got a telephone or a computer with a modem at your house, you can do all the banking you want without ever getting out of your pajamas.

If you're in a hurry and you want the easy way to manage your accounts, take advantage of telephone banking. If your bank is one of the few that doesn't offer this service, you might consider switching—most banks these days do offer this time-saving service.

If you've got a telephone and a PIN number (the same as your ATM card), you can join the telephone banking bunch. With telephone service, you can:

- Check your balances
- Find out which checks have cleared and which haven't
- Transfer funds from one account to another
- Order a new statement
- Get the latest interest quotes
- Stop payment on a check

If you're one of those people who buy their groceries with an ATM debit card and then forget to record the transaction or keep the receipt, telephone banking can

QUICK n' PAINLESS

All banks are not created equal when it comes to CD interest rates. Some federally insured banks with top safety ratings pay 1 to 2 percent more than others. To find these banks with the big pockets, check out this Web site:

http://www.bankrate.com

Unless you're retired or you need money to pay for basics, reinvesting the interest from your accounts is an easy way to save more money. Plus, reinvesting this "found" money can be automatic with CDs, mutual funds, and many stocks.

be a real sanity-saver. You'll always know what checks have cleared, what your balance is, and whether or not your Aunt Louise's birthday bonus has finally been deposited.

Navigating Internet Banking

While telephone banking is a boon, it can still take time to work your way through the recorded messages guiding you through the maze of banking possibilities. ("Press one to access your checking account. . . press two to access your savings account. . . "). Those of you with even less time to kill can fly through your banking chores if you have access to the Internet. We'll go into this in more depth in Chapter 16, but when it comes to saving time, banking on the World Wide Web makes a lot of sense. You may get an economic bonus with these banks—their low overhead means they have low costs and high interest rates.

To find out if your own bank has an Internet presence, search the bank's name with one of the many Internet search engines, such as Yahoo or Infoseek.

EMERGENCY FUNDS

Next, you'll want to keep some "emergency" money on hand so that when your truck's fuel pump goes, you won't have to charge the repairs on your credit card at 20 percent interest. Your emergency money should be easy to get to, lying in an interest-bearing account of some type, a very short-term CD, or U.S. Treasury bills. Try to have between three and six months' salary stashed away. Liquidity is certainly important, but you don't have to put all your money in a savings account in order to be able to sleep at night. In fact, there's as much liquidity with mutual funds or most stocks as with CDs, because if you need your money you can always sell the investments. (The risk here, of course, is that they may have temporarily decreased in value.) You could put your money in:

- A money market mutual fund, which usually pays more than a savings account and lets you get to your money simply by writing a check.

- U.S. Treasury bills (T bills), which usually pay more interest than savings accounts and are easily sold. Even better, you can buy short-term T bills that are timed to come due when you need the money, such as in 13 or 26 weeks.

- Stock mutual funds, which provide significantly better returns and can be liquidated at their current value if you need the money.

Of course, all your investments don't have to be liquid, especially if you plan major purchases or postpone expected bills for when one of your investments is coming due. If you're looking to buy a new van, for example, wait until the next CD comes due.

How much you invest depends on your disposable income, your retirement needs, whether you have college needs, and so on. It's terrific if you can save 10 percent of your annual income. However, too many people live paycheck to paycheck and don't invest anything. Start small and increase the amount when you receive raises, gifts, or bonuses.

QUICK **n** PAINLESS

To find out more about online banking, check out Security First Network Bank at http://www.sfnb. com—the first online bank.

Getting Time on Your Side

	The Old Way	The Lazy Way
Checking your account balance	30 minutes	5 minutes
Researching investments	3 hours	20 minutes
Finding out if a check has cleared	30 minutes	5 minutes
Choosing an account	1 hour	20 minutes
Transfer funds	30 minutes	5 minutes
Check interest rates	1 hour	5 minutes

The Carefree Way to Control Credit

Odds are nothing is quite as helpful to the lazy lifestyle as a credit card. It's so much easier to plunk down your American Express than it is to unearth your checkbook, find a pen, write out the check, record the transaction in your check register, and then hope you have enough money in your account to cover it.

If it's effortlessness you're seeking, credit cards are the answer. But there's a flip side to all this simplicity. Those of you who tend to reach for the plastic first and worry about paying later will find that this aspect of the lazy lifestyle has its down side. If you plunge in over your head with credit card debt, you'll spend far too much time juggling your finances to pay the bills. If you get behind with payments, you'll spend more time trying to repair your damaged credit report. And then you'll have to waste even more time explaining to bankers, potential employers, and apartment leasing companies why your credit report has more red ink than the federal budget.

Remember that buying something with a credit card is definitely the lazy way to handle money—as long as you really are handling money, and not trying to make yourself feel good by purchasing things today that you can't pay for tomorrow.

WATCH OUT FOR THOSE INTEREST RATES!

If you do use a credit card, odds are you've noticed that teeny tiny print at the bottom of the bill announcing the astronomical interest rates that come along with the package. Rates are so high, in fact, that you'll probably be paying off your wedding rehearsal dinner after your kids have graduated from college.

The average American carries about $3,900 worth of credit card debt every year. At 18 percent interest, if you pay the minimum due every month (usually 2 percent of the balance), it will take you (are you ready?) almost 36 years to repay, and cost you more than $10,000 in interest. (And that's if you never charge another thing on that card!) However, if you add just $10 a month to your payment, your debt will be paid off within seven years. Sounds amazing, but it's true.

Now let's look at how paying in bigger increments each month can pay off. If you owe $6,000 at 19 percent interest, and you pay $100 a month until the card is paid off and never charge another item, it will take you 21 years to pay off the debt. If you add just $10 to that each month, you can pay off the debt in less than 12 years. If you pay $200 each month, the debt will be gone in less than four years. Paying off the debt at $500 a month erases the problem in just over one year.

CREDIT CARD PROTECTION: DOES IT REALLY MAKE SENSE?

So there you are, adding a few dollars extra to your credit card bills each month and figuring you're home free. But what happens if somebody steals your credit card or ATM debit card? Most likely, if you're breathing and paying taxes, you've gotten lots of attention from folks who want you to buy credit card protection to cover your losses should your card ever be stolen and used by someone else.

Filling out all those forms and paying for extra protection may appeal to some people, but it's not for lazy money managers. You'll be happy to know you don't really need to fuss with this service.

It doesn't make much sense to pay for protection, since you are liable for a maximum loss of only $50 per lost card anyway. If you notify the companies before the cards are used, you aren't liable for anything.

There is an exception to this rule, however. If you're carrying around a fistful of credit cards—we're talking more than 10—you may not mind paying an annual fee for credit protection service that saves you from spending a couple of hours on the phone canceling each and every card in the event of a stolen wallet. If the thought of having to deal with 42 automated answering services leaves you with a migraine, you might be one of those few who would be better off with credit protection

IF YOU'RE SO
INCLINED

Some credit cards offer much lower interest rates than others. To get a list of low-rate cards (at a small fee), call RAM Research at 800-344-7714 or the Bankcard Holders of America at 703-389-5445.

service. It costs a bit, but it saves time, aggravation, and sore fingers from all that number-punching.

HASSLE-FREE CREDIT BUILDING

What if you don't have any credit to protect? There are some good, easy, and painless ways to build up your credit. Applying for every credit card come-on that crosses your doorstep isn't one of them. It takes an awful lot of time and energy to fill out all those forms, and even more time and energy to keep track of all those different accounts.

Having 35 cards may impress your friends, but it doesn't build a good credit history and it takes far more time to deal with than you probably have. In fact, having a large number of credit lines available can work against you when you apply for credit. The bank isn't going to be impressed that you have the ability to lay your hands on a pile of money; they're going to wonder what will happen to your mortgage payment if you actually charge up to the limit on every card you own. When you apply for a loan, a bank will assume that if you have a card with a $5,000 credit limit—even if there is no balance on the card—to all intents and purposes, you owe $5,000.

But just as it's important not to apply for every credit card that falls into the mailbox, it is important to apply for at least one. Credit in your own name is of vital importance. For those of us for whom time is at a premium, one of the best ways to simplify our lives is to get credit in our own name.

If your husband died and you don't have credit in your own name, for example, the bank can yank your

YOU'LL THANK YOURSELF LATER

Decide on the number of cards you want to apply for, and throw out all those other credit come-ons. A department store card or two, a gas card, and one major credit card should do it.

joint credit card quicker than you can say "don't leave home without it." Of course, after they've taken your card, you have the opportunity to apply for credit in your name. But if you don't have a credit history, you don't have a snowball's chance in a skillet of getting a card in your name.

If you think it's less of a hassle not to have credit in your name, you haven't been paying attention. Drop what you're doing and pick up the phone. Contact a company where you and your spouse have a joint account, and ask for an account in your name alone. The Equal Credit Opportunity Act requires that if you're married, you must be allowed to apply for credit in your own name and you can't be denied credit, as long as your credit history is satisfactory.

CREDIT EXPRESS: DIVE INTO THE WORLD WIDE WEB!

Of course, if you call a company by phone, you'll likely have to dictate the answers to a long list of credit questions, or you'll be asked to fill out an application form. More time frittered away.

If you're looking for the lazy way to manage your credit, there's no easier way than by hopping online and cruising the World Wide Web. Point your browser to the closest bank and you'll find instant access and helpful information. We'll go into this in more detail in Chapter 16, but if you have a computer and Internet access, fire up that modem and get cracking! You'll find an astonishing number of banks and credit card companies

A COMPLETE WASTE OF TIME

The 3 Worst Things to
Do with Your Credit:

1. Not have any.

2. Have too many cards.

3. Only have credit in
   your spouse's name.

online, and they'll be happy to have you apply for a card online.

IF YOU'RE TURNED DOWN FOR CREDIT. . .

If you get turned down for a loan on that brand-new blue Porsche you've got your heart set on, the lender has to tell you why you were denied, and the credit reporting agency must provide a free copy of the report to you. You can then review your report and verify if the data is accurate. If it isn't—and you'd be surprised how often it's not—you should work to have the incorrect information removed from the report, which we'll talk about a bit later on.

Drowning in Debt

Maybe you didn't get that Porsche because you have lousy credit. You've been so successful at getting credit cards that that now you're in over your head, and you can't pay all the bills that are pouring in.

If you find yourself in this situation, the first thing you need to do is prepare a list of all your outstanding balances. Most people are surprised to learn their debts are not quite as bad as they thought. If you've done this and you're still conscious, here's the lazy way to getting a handle on your debt:

- Do something about the problem today. Thinking about it tomorrow may have worked for Scarlett O'Hara, but it won't work for you.

- Cut expenses. It worked for Congress, and it can work for you.

- Make a repayment plan.

- Sell a major asset that really isn't necessary. If you have two cars, sell one. Sell your Microsoft stock or Aunt Agatha's collection of matchbox cars, but sell something.

- Withdraw money from an IRA. Although you're using future security, don't ruin your credit today for a rainy tomorrow 20 years from now.

- Get a home equity line of credit.

- Refinance your mortgage and consolidate outstanding loans.

- Borrow from family.

- Borrow from a bank.

- Borrow against the cash value of your life insurance policies.

Face Your Creditors

You can try to ignore your creditors, hide under your bed, and take the phone off the hook, but that involves an awful lot of energy. The lazy way to deal with this situation is the most straightforward. Tell your creditors in writing that you can't make a payment. Close the account so there are no further charges—before the creditor has a chance to close it for you. From there, work out a plan to repay the loan.

You'd be surprised at the number of folks who have credit difficulties but who refuse to acknowledge that they have a problem handling money. For many of us, how we handle money is intricately intertwined with

YOU'LL THANK YOURSELF LATER

Sit down today and find out how you can clean up your debt by using these tips, and you'll sleep much better tonight.

how we view ourselves. Often, people with problems handling money either never learned how when they were young or are using finances as a way to deal with other problems. If you're going to get a handle on your credit difficulties, you have to realize you've got a problem.

If you're still denying there's anything wrong, take this test:

- Do you often spend more than you earn?
- Are you forced to make day-to-day purchases on credit?
- Can you make only the minimum payments on monthly credit cards?
- If you lost your job, would you have trouble paying next month's bills?

"Yes" to any of these questions means that you've got a money handling problem. "Yes" to more than one suggests you should run, not walk, to your nearest credit counselor.

The Lowdown on Credit Reports

If you do have problems with money, chances are it's going to be reflected in a less-than-impressive credit file. Those of you who are worried about what Big Brother may be saying about your credit need to understand that the best way to deal with these fears is the straightforward way. It may seem easy to ignore potential problems, but eventually those problems will blow up in your face and require 10 times as much time and energy to repair.

IF YOU'RE SO
INCLINED

Those of you who can't stop spending may want to contact Debtors Anonymous (similar to Alcoholics Anonymous) at General Services Building, P.O. Box #400, New York, NY 10163-0400, or call 212-642-8220. Find the group closest to your home.

The information in your credit file is very important and its accuracy imperative. Here is where you'll find information about any late payments, your credit history, nonpayment, and past foreclosures.

It doesn't take a lot of energy to keep tabs on this file. All you have to do is review your credit report once a year. Put it on your calendar the week of April 15, when money is on your mind. If that date is too painful, then write it down January 1, as a good way to start off a new year.

The three main companies that maintain information on your credit are:

- TRW Credit Data/Consumer Assistance
- Equifax Credit Services
- Trans Union Credit Information Services

IF YOU'RE SO
INCLINED

Before you buy a home or take out a loan, be sure to ask for a copy of your report to prevent problems due to overlooked errors.

Fixing What's Wrong

If you don't have lots of time to spare sitting around writing letters and explaining away that bad credit, you'll want to make sure you fix everything that's incorrect in that report, as soon as possible.

Though it may seem like the ideal lazy solution, do not hire a credit correction company to clear up your credit file. For a fee, these services promise to correct your credit report, but it's actually very easy to solve the problem yourself. Put that checkbook back in your pocket and correct the problem yourself with these easy steps:

- Contact the companies by certified mail, stating the incorrect information. Request they investigate.

- If you haven't heard within 60 days, send another letter reminding them that they are required by law to investigate incorrect information or provide an updated credit report with the inaccurate information removed from your report.

Unfortunately, there may be negative information on your credit report that is perfectly correct. You can't make a silk purse out of a shoe box, and you can't wave a wand and transform negative information if it's correct, however much you might like to. If you are trying to repair your credit history, work with your creditor. A negative remark lasts for seven years and bankruptcy hangs around for ten. If you find information on your record that's older than this, you should be able to have it removed.

If you suddenly inherit money or simply decide to mend your ways and start repaying your bills promptly, in about two to three years the tenor of your credit report should begin to change.

It may seem tempting, but you shouldn't hire anyone who says he can get you a brand-new "clean" credit report. Improving your credit history by changing your federal identification number isn't lazy, it's against the law. Your history is your history. You can't erase it, but you can start today in building a better credit report. Here's the lazy way to better credit:

- Cut up your cards.

- Pay in cash, and don't overspend.
- Establish a realistic budget and stick to it.
- Establish a plan to get out of debt.
- Negotiate a repayment plan with creditors.
- Establish a cushion for emergencies.
- Don't job hop.

Some of you with shaky credit may have gotten offers for secured credit cards from banks, who offer to give you a card with a credit limit equal to the amount you deposit in their bank. It's perfectly legal and may be a way for those of you with poor credit history to get a card.

The bad news: There are often fees charged to open such an account, and you don't usually receive competitive money market interest rates on the funds held in the secured account. Still, it's a way to begin a credit history, and it's often possible to convert this account to a standard card.

As if there isn't enough to worry about when it comes to credit, it's also possible to have too many cards. Most of us receive tons of credit card offers in the mail promising low interest rates, high credit limits, and easy availability. If you take all the cards that come in, you'll have too much credit. The high limits can hurt you when you go to get a loan, since lenders want borrowers to have only 36 percent of their gross income as debt. All you need are one or two gasoline cards, a few department store credit cards, one or two major cards, and a debit card.

YOU'LL THANK YOURSELF LATER

When you open the secured account, ask if and when it can be converted to a standard account. Put that date on your calendar so you can make the conversion as soon as possible.

BANKRUPTCY: DOES IT REALLY MAKE LIFE EASIER?

Many people who teeter on the brink of insolvency may have the idea that declaring bankruptcy is the lazy way out of a financial black hole. Wrong! Declaring bankruptcy is a monumental headache. If you don't have time to water your plants and walk the dog, you absolutely will not have time to deal with all of the hassles that come along with a bankruptcy petition.

If possible, try working with the Consumer Credit Counseling Service, a national nonprofit organization that helps you prepare a repayment plan. A trained counselor will help you come up with a budget to maintain your basic living expenses and outline options for addressing your total financial situation. If creditors are hassling you, a counselor can negotiate with them to repay your debts through a financial management plan. Under this plan, creditors may agree to reduce payments or drop fees. After starting the plan, you deposit money with CCCS each month to cover these new negotiated payment amounts. Then CCCS will distribute this money to your creditors to repay your debts. The service charges approximately nine dollars a month, so be wary of companies with similar names and promises who charge a much heftier fee.

There are more than 1,100 CCCS locations nationwide, supported mainly by contributions from community organizations, financial institutions, and merchants.

Contact the Consumer Credit Counseling Service at 8611 2nd Avenue, Suite 100, Silver Spring, MD 20910, or call 800-388-2227 (available 24 hours a day).

However, there are a few people who may do better with a bankruptcy filing. If you don't have many assets, have a lot of debt, and have income that barely covers monthly debt payments, bankruptcy may be an option.

If you've already made up your mind to file and you have major assets to protect, you may want to hire an attorney to help you. But remember where the advice to file for bankruptcy comes from: An attorney who earns a legal fee from doing bankruptcy filings may have a conflict of interest, since filing for bankruptcy generates fees. On the other hand, the Consumer Credit Counseling Service (a nonprofit educational service) is funded by credit card companies. These counselors may therefore not be anxious to recommend bankruptcy.

If you're behind in your credit card payments and you're being hassled by the company, send them a written notice demanding that they stop calling. Remember, the only way the agency can really get satisfaction is to file a lawsuit. Everything else they do is designed to get you to pay so they don't have to go to court. If the company doesn't stop calling, send a letter to the Federal Trade Commission with documentation of the times and dates of the calls, with a copy to the credit card company.

Those of you who don't have the energy to pay attention to your credit limits should know that most

Congratulations! You gotten your credit under control! Now take a break and go relax with hot cocoa in front of a roaring fire. You've earned it.

The Lazy Way

companies allow you to charge only about 10 percent above your limit before freezing your card. Rather than risking embarrassment by approaching this limit, request a credit limit increase. It's better to increase your limit before you charge than to make the request after you've tiptoed over the line.

If you feel that credit cards are not one of your weaknesses, increasing your limit is a good option. But if your plastic gets a lot of play, you should consider keeping an eye on your balance instead. Take a good look at your monthly statement and see if you need to exercise a bit more control.

Getting Time on Your Side

	The Old Way	The Lazy Way
Applying for a credit card	2 weeks	1 day
Getting a copy of your credit file	2 weeks	5 minutes
Getting a list of lower-rate cards	2 weeks	10 minutes
Paying your bills	30 minutes	10 minutes
Reducing debt	Years	Months
Choosing the card that's right for you	2 hours	10 minutes

Chapter eight

Painlessly Pocket That Change! Saving Money Around the House

Your household expenses cover more than you might think—phone bills, clothing, food, the car, even haircuts! Cell phones, Porsches, designer jeans, and Beluga caviar may separate the Joneses from everybody else, but what good are all those things if you're worried about being carted off to debtors' prison at the end of the month?

If you want to start having a little bit of extra change left over, it pays to conserve. Unless you're counting on that phone call from Steven Spielberg about your audition for his next movie, remember this: It's easier to spend less than it is to earn more. Here's how!

FOOD FOR THOUGHT

One of the biggest areas of the budget for most folks is food, but there are lots of easy ways to save on it without spending lots of time.

A COMPLETE WASTE OF TIME

The 3 Worst Things to Do with Your Food Budget:

1. Eat out every night because you don't have time to cook.

2. Shop when you're hungry.

3. Drive to three different stores to save 10 cents on a package of meat.

- Always compare unit prices.

- Instead of paying extra for "low-fat" cheeses, simply buy regular cheese (or other food) and use less, or cut it yourself with unflavored bread crumbs.

- Try store brands of some items. Will you really notice the difference between store-brand and premium-brand white vinegar, for example?

- Cut the amount of meat you use; you don't *have* to add a pound of meat to every recipe. Instead of planning meals around meat, make vegetables, pasta, or rice the main course; use meat as a side dish.

- Avoid juice boxes—put juice in thermoses.

- Buy large bags of rice; cook more than you need and refrigerate the rest. Reheating rice takes just a few moments in a microwave, so you've saved money and time.

- Buy generic cereal in plastic bags.

- In summer, buy extra amounts of vegetables and freeze excess.

- Use canned foods to save money.

- Shop at superstores such as Sam's Club, PriceCostco, and others. You can save up to 40 percent without the hassle of clipping coupons.

EXTENDED WARRANTIES: WHAT HAVE THEY DONE FOR YOU LATELY?

If you want to save money around the house, one of the easiest ways is to just say "no" when the salesclerk waves that "extended warranty" contract in your face. A lot of people don't realize that most breakdowns are caused by defects that are covered under the standard manufacturer's warranty. Besides, wear and tear, or even outright damage (as when Junior stuffs his Pop Tart into the VCR) isn't covered by most extended warranties anyway. If you avoid extended warranties, you save as much as 30 percent of the sticker price. All without lifting a finger! Isn't this easy?

PHONE CENTS: DIAL UP A SMALLER PHONE BILL

Ever since Solomon divided up Ma Bell, figuring out how to save money with the phone system has been a real challenge for money managers looking to save time. But don't give up, there are some easy ways to manage!

First of all, nobody should be leasing a phone these days. The phone that you can buy in a store for $20 may cost you $77 a year to lease—every year. Fancier models cost even more. Yet 10 million Americans are still leasing their phones. It's not a good way to save money. It's also more time-consuming than simply buying a phone.

Companies will tell you that leasing protects you against phone damage—you get a free phone if your leased phone breaks. But phones are one of the last technological miracles of the 20th century; they're among

YOU'LL THANK YOURSELF LATER

According to *Consumer Reports*, more than 95 percent of people who buy extended warranties on appliances and electronics never use them.

If you share the phone bill with another, or need to separate calls, ask your carrier for access code service. This lets you dial a code before a long-distance number that automatically itemizes your bill by access code.

those few products that rarely break down. If you're still worried about breakdowns, consider this: You can easily buy two phones for less than the cost of a year's lease. You could buy a new phone every year and still be paying less than you would for an annual lease.

Read on for some more quick phone tips:

- If you phone home often when you're out of town, consider getting a personal 800 or 888 number; it's usually cheaper (14 to 19 cents per minute) than a calling card (27 to 38 cents per minute).

- For short long-distance calls, a prepaid phone card is almost always better than a calling card. The per-minute rate is higher, but you won't pay any surcharge.

- No time to wait? Bypass tedious computerized answering systems by pressing 0. This usually connects you with an operator.

- Use a provider who offers billing in six-second increments, especially if you make lots of brief calls.

- Instead of a second phone line for a home business, opt for a second ring service on the same line.

CAR CENTS: DRIVING A BETTER BARGAIN

It may seem as if leasing a car is simpler than jousting with your local car salesman, but in fact it's just as tedious to lease a car as it is to buy one. Think carefully about which option is better for you.

You'll do better leasing a car if you tend to get a new car every couple of years anyway, or if your employer subsidizes your lease. However, unless you have very good credit, you're better off buying a used car, since you need a higher credit rating in order to lease. Remember that the longer you keep a leased car, the greater the chance that you may interfere with the car's residual value. The residual value is the agreed-on value of the car after you've leased it. If the dealer feels poor maintenance or too many miles have eroded that value, you could be in trouble. If you tend to put lots of miles on a car, leasing may not be for you; most leases limit your mileage to 12,000 miles per year.

For a quick rundown on the pros and cons of leasing a car, check this out:

Pros

- Many leases don't require a down payment.
- You may be able to lease a more expensive car than you could afford to buy.
- You don't have to worry about reselling the car when the lease expires.

Cons

- When your lease expires, you may have to pay "disposition charges" (the dealer's cost of auctioning your car).
- The total cost of leasing is almost always more than buying a car with cash—and usually more expensive than borrowing the money to buy a car.

QUICK n' PAINLESS

If you really want to save time and money, check out public transportation. It's cheaper, it cuts down wear and tear on your car, and you can work or read while someone else does the driving!

- When the lease expires, you're left with nothing.

- Almost every lease comes with mileage limits; if you go over the limit, you pay a penalty (as much as 15 cents a mile).

- You still have to pay for insurance and maintenance.

Another easy way to save your pennies is to buy average-grade gas, since in most cases premium gas doesn't make your car run better—at least, not enough that you would notice. Experts say that a higher-grade gas may improve your car's fuel economy or performance, but the change is so slight you won't be able to tell the difference. Both domestic and foreign cars are now designed to operate efficiently with 87-octane gas. Many also are equipped with sensors that automatically adjust your engine to eliminate knocks. Only if you drive a high-performance car (Porsche, Mercedes, or Corvette, for example) do you still need premium gas.

PAYING THE LANDLORD LESS—IT IS POSSIBLE!

If you're renting a house, you may assume that there's not much you can do about saving money here. That may not be true. Try renting a larger place with a roommate—this also means there's someone else around to help with housework!

If you don't want to share your place, try negotiating your rental increases as they come up each year. If your living quarters are deteriorating—your landlord hasn't fixed that leaky faucet or replaced the torn rugs—you have more leverage. If you pay your rent on time and don't throw loud parties, then you're a good tenant, and your landlord won't want to lose you. (It's a lot of hassle to find a new renter!)

Now let's look at utilities. If you pay for your trash pickup by the number of cans out there, recycle! You'll save on garbage pickup, and there will be fewer heavy cans to lug out to the curb. Install water flow regulators on toilets and shower heads. Turn off lights when you leave the room and replace old, power-draining appliances.

CLOTHING AND ACCESSORIES

When you buy clothing, check the label. That dreamy dress might be on sale, but if you have to pack it off to the cleaners every time you wear it, it's going to cost big after a few years. Stick to machine-washable fabrics.

While you're at it, buy classic, not trendy. You'll be able to keep your clothes for a long time and really get your money's worth. Besides, it takes time to hit the mall a couple of times a year to stock up on the newest fashions.

Now check out the accessories, such as shoes, purses, and jewelry. They can cost a lot, especially if you have a different set for each outfit. Do you really need that many? Try to consolidate, and buy only what you really need. If you buy quality items, they should last for years.

QUICK **n** *PAINLESS*

Go through your closet and weed out any items you haven't worn for three years. Take the clothes to a yard sale if you have the time, or a consignment shop if you don't. Invest the money you earn.

VACATIONS

We all need time off to recharge our batteries, but it's important to remember that a vacation isn't an investment: Don't put it on your credit card if you can't pay it off right away. If you can't take a vacation without charging it, then you can't afford it. Do you really want to pay for that week of relaxation for the next two years?

Just because you can't afford to go to Paris this year doesn't mean you have to stay home and pout. Try camping at a national park in your state. Stay home and tour all the sites within 50 miles that you've always wanted to visit but never had the time to.

If you do decide to travel, consider off-season vacations. Most people think about going to the islands in the dead of winter, but a trip to St. Martin in July is much more reasonable—and the temperature actually stays about the same year round. Enjoy, and save money!

Keep your eye peeled for "bought but can't use" advertisements for tickets in your local paper, and sign up with online travel services that keep you apprised of the latest cheapest fares.

PERSONAL CARE

When it comes to getting your hair cut, you can spend big for that look you love. If you really believe your stylist is worth more than $100, try going to a discount place in between cuts for maintenance. Or you can really save (while taking a risk) by getting your hair cut at a local beauty school.

Exercise is always a good deal, and in the long run it may well save on health care costs, too, but you don't need a high-priced club to get the exercise you need. Check out community centers (many offer fitness programs) and local colleges and schools (for running tracks, tennis courts, swimming pools, and so on). And what's to stop you from simply lacing up your Nikes and heading out for a run around the park? Set up a volleyball net in your backyard and play with family members. Buy some basic gym equipment for home (you can often find it in good condition at yard sales, sold by other folks who had big ideas and no time).

Medical Care

If there's one thing that's subject to rapid changes in the United States these days, it's the health care scene. Still, there are some basics you can keep in mind:

- Always get a second opinion for any major surgery.
- Don't buy more health care coverage than you actually need.
- If you must take drugs for a chronic problem, consider buying them through a mail-order company.

Studies have shown that a good course of brief psychotherapy can save you money down the road in reduced medical costs. The good news is that counseling does *not* have to last for 10 years to be effective. Many kinds of mental health care providers offer "short-term counseling." If you think this might be helpful to you, your provider should be able to tell you honestly how many sessions therapy may take.

QUICK n' PAINLESS

To find less expensive drugs, try:

- Family Pharmaceuticals of America (800-922-3444)
- Pharmail Corp. (800-237-8927)
- Retired Persons Services, Inc. (AARP) (800-456-2277)

Getting Time on Your Side

	The Old Way	The Lazy Way
Buying medicines	1 hour	5 minutes
Getting a phone	30 minutes (leasing)	10 minutes (buying)
Exercising	2 hours (at a gym)	45 minutes (at home)
Sorting out joint phone bills	1 hour	2 minutes
Cleaning your clothing	1 day	1 hour
Buying groceries	3 hours	30 minutes

A Mind Is a Terrible Thing to Waste

It was only yesterday that your daughter was sleeping peacefully in the hospital's newborn nursery, and you were wondering how on earth you were going to pay for college. Now she's trying on her mortarboard, and you still don't know if you can afford tuition. Somehow, you never had the spare cash to squirrel away, or the time to figure out the best way to do it.

You're not alone. Not everyone is in a position to start saving the instant a child is born. If your son is already in second grade and you haven't built much of a nest egg, it's not too late. If your daughter is a senior in high school, it's still not too late. (It's harder, but it's not hopeless.)

In fact, it's never too late. The important thing, wherever you are, is to stop right now and figure out where you stand and how you can reach your goal. If your child is still small, you can figure out how much you have to save each month to reach your goal in 10, 12, or 18 years. If your child is almost ready to graduate, you'll need to focus on paying now. Either

For an overview of online college financial aid, organizations, scholarship databases, and contact information for financial aid offices, check out http://www.finaid.org or http://www.collegboard.org/css/html/proform.html.

way, you need to look at some realistic goals so you can take action. Remember: A goal is not a wish but a statement of purpose, so it should be as concrete and specific as possible.

The easy way to figure out how you're going to pay for college is to get a computer program to help you. Try one of these:

- The College Board's "How to Pay for College" ($17) is a Windows program that includes a general overview of financial aid, a loan payment calculator, and a family contribution estimator. The disk comes free with the College Board's *College Costs and Financial Aid Handbook*. For more information, call 212-713-8165.

- John Hancock College Savings Plus Program is a free, no-obligation interactive computer program designed to help families plan for their kids' college education. The software shows an estimate of future tuition, room, and board costs at more than 1,500 public and private schools based on the year the child expects to begin attending. For more information, call 800-633-1809, or e-mail to marstonpr@mcimail.com.

- Smart Plan ($35) is a college financial planning software package that includes a tuition database for more than 1,000 colleges and universities and an online investment guide tailored to college fund investing. For more information, call 800-642-5750, or e-mail smrtplan@csra.net.

- Tufro ($28) is a Tooth and Money Saving Kit that helps parents and children save teeth and money at the same time. The kit uses the experience of losing baby teeth to educate children about proper dental care and to encourage families to save and invest for their children's college education, all at the same time. The kit includes tooth calculator software, a set of Toothvelopes for saving baby teeth, a Tooth Box, and a booklet that describes the Toothaccount program. For more information, call 888-HI-TUFRO.

The good news is that you don't need all of the money available when your child starts college. Remember that college is a four-year process, so you won't need to have all the funds available the September of your child's freshman year. You should also note that you can continue to pay for college after your child graduates. This helps make the costs more palatable.

The best way to save is to contribute to a college fund from every paycheck or make a contribution monthly. Looking at college savings as a type of fixed monthly payment guarantees that the money will be deposited. It's often hard to find money to contribute, so the payments should be part of your monthly bill payment process. Or put any income tax refund into a college account. It's interesting to see how quickly the funds accumulate if the savings are made with each paycheck, each month, or annually when you receive a lump sum refund. Start small, if necessary, and increase the savings as you can afford more.

QUICK ⏱ PAINLESS

For a fast way to guesstimate the cost of college, take the four-year tuition and divide it by the months you have until your child is ready for college. This will give you the ballpark figure you will need to save each month.

Save whatever you can. If you can afford to save $300 a month, do it. If you can save only $50 a month, then do that. Too many people have an "all or nothing" approach to savings: Unless they can put away at least $100 a month, they figure it's not worth it and so they don't save anything.

If your budget permits saving only five dollars a week, put that aside. Five dollars a week is $20 a month, which adds up to $240 a year. Save regularly. It's a statement of your faith in your children's future.

So how do you know how much to save? The amount needed depends on whether your child eventually chooses a public or private school, but if you're earning only a modest income, aim for saving a third or half of the total cost. You can make up the rest with scholarships, grants, loans, and having your child work while going to school.

If all those details give you a headache, visit one of the many "calculators" online and let them do the figuring for you. You simply key in the type of school, your child's age, and presto! They'll tell you how much you need to save.

Let's say you invest $100 a month starting when your baby is born at a conservative interest rate of 8 percent. You will have $43,100 when that baby is ready to enter college at age 18. Although this may not cover all the expenses, it will make a nice dent in the bill.

Many folks say it's hard finding the discretionary income to put towards a college fund for a new baby. If you are a two-income household, most likely you have child care expenses. Once your child is old enough to go

YOU'LL THANK YOURSELF LATER

In fact, saving even the smallest amount is better than nothing. This savings will decrease the amount of loans you will need to incur when the time comes to pay for college.

to school, those expenses will stop. At that time, you could invest what you were paying the child care provider in your child's college account. This can add up to a significant savings over the years.

If one of you stayed home while your children were small and you went back to work when they entered elementary school, place a portion of that extra salary in a college fund. Since you weren't used to the extra income before, you could spend only a portion of the funds and save the difference.

Let's say you're already at the point where your child is a sophomore or junior in high school, and those college tuition bills are starting to inhabit your nightmares. It's time to get serious about your options: scholarships, fellowships, financial aid, and student loans.

You'll be happy to know that it's never too late to start saving and planning. First, here's what you do:

- Verify that the accounts and investments you have are earning the highest rate of return possible without significant risk.

- Make certain you are creditworthy, and if you need to borrow funds, make certain your credit history is accurate.

- Make sure you haven't tapped out your borrowing capacity. (It's often better to pay off high-interest loans than save at money market rates.)

Now it's time to learn about the various ways to pay for college. You could spend hours—days, actually—in the library looking up all this stuff, or you could either

IF YOU'RE SO
INCLINED

If you intend to sell stock to pay for your child's college expenses, put it in both parents' names. This way, you can give $20,000 to your child in one year without paying a gift tax.

buy some software or go online to find the answers in a matter of minutes. We bet we know which way you'll go.

To save money on an education, have your child:

- Go to a community college.

- Consider a program that lets her graduate in three years instead of four.

- Find out if any courses he took in high school transfer to college, possibly saving a semester or two of tuition.

- Attend summer classes at a college near your home to supplement the college year (make certain the courses are transferable before your child goes to the time and expense of taking them).

- Consider a work/study program that helps provide funds for tuition while she goes to school.

- Live at home and commute to classes, rather than living on campus.

- Attend college while employed. Many employers reimburse some or all tuition expenses for their employees.

SCHOLARSHIP SEARCH SOFTWARE

If your child is getting ready for college now, you need to be thinking about what you can do now to help handle the cost of college. Scholarships, grants, and fellowships don't need to be paid back, and so they are very attractive. When applying, look for out-of-the-way scholarships; don't apply just to those that everyone else knows

Many colleges permit payment through the installment plan: You pay the annual college cost through a 10-month payment plan. This is a good way to go if you don't have the money to pay the entire tuition bill.

about. Check out the Foundation Center (http://fdncenter.org) for offbeat organizations that offer money to scholars.

There are lots of lazy ways to figure all this out. If you have a computer, your search for information on college finances just got much easier. There is a range of useful software programs that can help you locate good scholarships. These include:

- The College Board's Fund Finder: The College Cost Explorer is a database of national, state, public, and private scholarship information from 3,300 places. There's a separate database of college costs and financial aid and 2,800 two- and four-year schools, and worksheets to calculate your contribution. The database is updated each year. It's expensive to own, but you can access a smaller version for free on the World Wide Web as ExPAN Scholarship Search. For more information, call 800-223-9726.

- Peterson's Award Search ($15) is a database of scholarships and grants from 1,900 sources. You can enter a profile to find a list of awards to match your interests. For information, call 800-338-3282.

- Cash for Class Version 2.0 is a Windows program that includes a searchable database of more than 10,000 sources of scholarships, fellowships, and awards on five disks. For more information, call or fax 714-673-9039.

- Pinnacle Peak Solutions (Scholarships 101) hones in on scholarships alone—more than 380,000 individual

Congratulations! You've used your computer to get information about scholarships the easy way, so go ahead! Play that game of solitaire!

The Lazy Way

scholarships worth more than $980 million. The database includes college-controlled aid and government aid, as well as scholarships from the private sector. A boon for the lazy money manager: The software can automatically print up request-for-information letters and mailing labels. For more information, call 800-762-7101.

FINANCIAL AID SOFTWARE

Financial aid is usually dependent on need. Many people fear that if they do save, those savings mean they won't qualify for aid. To a degree, this is true. However, your annual income has a much greater influence on how much aid you qualify for than how much money you've saved. Although the family who has saved for college may be required to contribute more towards a child's college expenses, two families with comparable incomes will be required to contribute fairly comparable payments. Moreover, the parents with savings won't have to borrow (or will have to borrow less) and thus will have a more secure future after their children have graduated from college. At the moment, the maximum amount that parents can be expected to contribute in a given year is less than 5.6 percent of their total assets. Home equity is not included.

There are some quick ways to find out about financial aid. Several of the most common sources of information are:

- the financial aid office of the college your child wants to attend

- a high school guidance office

- a local library

- bookstores

Of course, the very easiest and fastest ways are online. There are many scholarship search programs on the Internet; a good place to start is FastWEB (http://www.fastweb.com). Or check out these software programs for more information:

- College Financial Planners, Inc., sells The Fine Art of Negotiating a College Education software ($60), including a 64-page booklet that covers all aspects of college planning and negotiating, four separate negotiation letters for reference, and Quik-Plan software. The software includes a simple way to calculate how much money each college really expects the family to pay and a quick calculation of how much gift aid each of 1,800 schools is willing to award. For more information, call 714-573-7866 or e-mail CONCFPI@aol.com.

- KeyScape is free software from Key Education Resources, a collection of college financial aid planning tools including a loan payment and budgeting calculator and a college offer comparison calculator, a college planning calendar, and answers to frequently asked questions.

- Peterson's Financial Aid Planner ($27) is a set of MS-DOS financial aid calculators that includes both college cost and loan options calculators. For more information, call 800-338-3282.

YOU'LL THANK YOURSELF LATER

Have your child apply to a school that you *can* afford, such as a small state college, in addition to an expensive dream school. Then if your other financial aid packages fall through, your child will be able to afford to go somewhere. She can always transfer to the other school in the last year or two.

LOANS

The family's contribution to college must be paid each semester. This can equal a hefty sum. But fortunately, there's a way to manage this cost without taking out a high-interest commercial loan or cashing in retirement funds. You could try one of the government's loan programs—although they come with yards and yards of paperwork and all the other hassles attached to government programs.

You could choose a college with an innovative payment plan. Many schools offer loan programs for middle-income families. Other schools let you pay your family contribution in installments. Or you could try a commercial tuition payment plan, in which the commercial organization forwards the money to the school twice a year and then collects monthly payments from you. There's no interest, but you must start paying well before the tuition is due.

For an easy way to find such a plan, check out Tuition Management Systems, 4 John Clarke Road, Newport, RI 02842, 800-722-4867, or point your browser to http://www.afford.com.

Other commercial plans include:

- KNIGHT College Resource Group, 855 Boylston Street, Boston, MA 02116 (800-225-6783)

- Academic Management Services, 50 Vision Boulevard, East Providence, RI 02914 (800-635-0120)

- Education Credit Corp., 2252 Morello Avenue, Pleasant Hill, CA 94523 (800-477-4977)

TUITION PREPAYMENT PLAN

A tuition prepayment plan is an easy way to save for college if you're sure your child will want to go to one of your state's schools. This plan allows you to deposit money into an account for education at a college in your state, with the guarantee that the money you deposit will cover your child's education when she or he is of college age. The problem is, your child will then be restricted to attending a college in your state.

The good thing about these plans for the lazy money manager is that they are not hard to follow, and you won't have to spend lots of time trying to figure out how much to save if your kid should want to go to Harvard.

To help assess the strengths and weaknesses of these prepayment plans, the College Entrance Examination Board has issued a set of questions for you to keep in mind:

- Is there a minimum contribution required to enter the program? Are incremental additions possible?

- Is there a maximum annual amount that can be contributed? Will any such maximum restrict the accumulation below a realistic projection of future college costs?

- Can anyone in the family contribute? Are there exclusions?

- Can the proceeds from the plan be transferred to another family member if the child's educational plans change?

Is all this financial investigation starting to make you feel like Ebenezer Scrooge in his counting house? Relax. Put on your favorite CD, close your eyes, and visualize your child marching up to get that diploma!

The Lazy Way

- Are there eligibility restrictions—for example, can you apply only to a particular class of schools, such as only independent colleges? Are there penalties associated with these restrictions?

- Is the yield from the plan guaranteed? How? How are you protected from investment deficits below college cost levels?

- Is the plan insured? Can the investment be recovered if the plan sponsor ceases to exist?

- Does the plan cover all college costs or just tuition?

- Are there age restrictions or time limits on use? Do proceeds from the plan have to be used within a certain number of years after high school?

- Are there residency requirements for eligibility? What happens if you move during the plan years?

- How many years of study are covered by the proceeds? Is graduate school possible? Is part-time attendance possible?

- Are there restrictions as to who might match funds contributed to the plan? Could an employer or state contribute?

- What are the refund conditions if your child doesn't go to college for whatever reason?

- Do you benefit if there is more money in the fund than you need, or is the profit a bonus to the sponsor?

- Will the plan benefits be taxable, either for federal or state taxes? Will any tax accrue to the contributor, plan sponsor, or student?

IF YOU'RE SO
INCLINED

Tuition prepayment plans can be great, but make sure you read all of the fine print first!

Of course, lots of lazy money managers may find the prepayment plan interesting but may not like to be restricted to one college. If this is your situation, there's another option.

The College Savings Bank of Princeton allows you to invest in a CollegeSure CD, and they guarantee you will have enough to pay tuition when your child is ready for college. This plan is more flexible than state- or college-sponsored plans, since you're not committing to any one college.

The drawback: You need a large lump sum to contribute, and if you've got that much available you can probably earn more with a different kind of investment, such as a stock mutual fund.

EDUCATION IRA

Under the Taxpayer Relief Act of 1997, you can now withdraw funds from an IRA for educational expenses without incurring a 10-percent penalty, although the money you withdraw can be taxed. Parents can avoid even this tax liability by investing up to $500 a year in an IRA in their child's name (if the child is under age 18) and then withdrawing the funds for use towards college. Putting money into a child's educational IRA is a good idea, because it's neither taxed nor penalized when it is withdrawn to pay for college. If the child doesn't use her educational IRA, you can roll it over for use by another child.

YOU'LL THANK YOURSELF LATER

If your child is still small, you should invest a portion of your portfolio in zero coupon bonds that will mature when the student is ready to attend school and a blue chip or equity stock fund for long-term growth potential.

Drawbacks to the educational IRA include:

- Income limitation rules can get you from either direction—some disqualify you if you make too much, some disqualify you if you make too little.

- You can't have an educational IRA and participate in a tuition prepayment plan for your child.

- The IRA will be considered a part of your child's assets, and thus be included in the 35 percent figure that must be paid from the child's assets before financial aid is considered.

APPLYING ELECTRONICALLY

A few schools are jumping on the computer bandwagon in a big way—some even offer a scholarship contest as an incentive for those who apply electronically. Check these out for applying the lazy way:

- CollegeNET provides Web-based electronic application to more than 40 schools, along with a scholarship database.

- CollegeEdge lets you apply to 166 colleges and universities. If you submit your application to one of the seven schools that accept electronic applications, you are entered into a drawing for a $1,000 scholarship. SNAP Technologies (the company that sells CollegeEdge) also offers a $1,000 SNAP scholarship. At the CollegeEdge Web site (http://www.snapweb.

com) you can find a college search database, basic information about financial aid, and a list of FAQs from the Ask CollegeEdge service. For more information, e-mail webmaster@snapweb.com.

- CollegeLink supports electronic submission of applications to more than 800 colleges; some have reduced or dropped application fees for those who use CollegeLink to apply. The first application is free, but there is a five-dollar charge to CollegeLink for the rest; you send back the disk to CollegeLink to finish the process. CollegeLink transmits the applications electronically to the schools and sends you a copy of the application printed on the school's application form. E-mail collink@collegelink.com for more information.

- Collegescape lets you print applications to more than 200 colleges and grad schools for free; more than 50 of these schools will waive application fees for those who submit their applications this way. The Collegescape Web site includes a college search database. For more information, call 888-206-6297 or e-mail information@collegescape.com.

A COMPLETE WASTE OF TIME

The 3 Worst Things to Do When Applying for College:

1. Overlook fee waiver options.

2. Send in applications late.

3. Send in incomplete paperwork.

Getting Time on Your Side

	The Old Way	The Lazy Way
Finding out about scholarships	2 weeks	1 day
Calculating costs	1 hour	5 minutes
Figuring financial aid	1 day	1 hour
Applying	2 weeks	1 day
Researching schools	Months	A few weeks
Fill out financial aid forms	2 weeks	2 days

Chapter ten

Everyone's Gotta Pay – Taxes

Taxes. Who's got time for all that paperwork? If you're like most folks, you get a migraine at the mere thought of gathering up all those receipts, decoding the tax forms, and trying to figure out if your kid's campaign to save the whales counts as a charity.

You'll be happy to know there's an easier way to hack your way through the IRS jungle: It's called Hiring a Tax Preparer. Some of you out there really do need to call in the cavalry to prepare your tax forms. When your returns become complicated or cumbersome (when you stop using the short form, perhaps) you might want to get help preparing your return.

You'll be surprised how often a tax preparer knows of new deductions that you haven't heard about. Plus, wouldn't you rather sit back, put your feet up and sip a Dr. Pepper, and let your preparer stay up till midnight refiguring your depreciation on that new computer system you bought?

Having someone else do the math is truly the lazy way to prepare your taxes. But if the promise of saving time and energy hasn't convinced you to hire a tax expert, there's a quick way to decide if you might benefit from extra help. It's a good idea to have your taxes prepared by a professional if you:

- are self-employed
- use the long form
- have bought or sold a home this year
- have business expenses, car expenses, or depreciation
- have rental property

If you do choose to get help preparing your taxes, you'll be faced with the problem of wondering whom to hire. Remember that just about anyone can hang out a "tax preparer" shingle. You don't need any formal education or certification to start doing tax returns, or any fancy degrees after your name.

If tax preparers work for a tax preparation firm (such as H&R Block), odds are they have had some training. The company may have educational requirements for the preparers they hire. Of course, there are several different types of tax experts. If your expert says she is a tax preparer, that means her job is to prepare your tax return according to law, to the best of her ability. Tax preparers just stick to the facts; they don't give advice.

A tax planner or tax adviser, on the other hand, prepares your return and helps analyze and advise how you can save on your taxes. A tax adviser should help you find the best investments for your tax situation.

Then there's an "enrolled agent," a tax preparer who specializes in tax preparation. Enrolled agents must pass a four-part, 12-hour test showing they have the knowledge required to prepare returns. Continuing education is required to maintain the enrolled agent designation.

Or, you might choose a certified public accountant (CPA), a professional who meets certain educational requirements and has passed the Uniform CPA exam administered by the American Institute of Certified Public Accountants. CPAs must complete a certain number of continuing education courses to maintain their certification.

If you're doing extensive, comprehensive estate planning, or if you need advice on a complicated tax matter, your best bet is to consult a tax attorney. A tax attorney is a lawyer who also has earned a master's degree in taxation.

READ ALL ABOUT IT

Of course, some of you may resent having to pay someone else just to figure out how much you need to pay the government. If you're determined to save the fee and do it yourself, there are shortcuts you may find helpful. Yes, Virginia, there is a lazy way to do your taxes. But remember—your tax-preparer's fee is also tax deductible.

The government has some information that can help you. In fact, the government has lots of information: more than 500 free publications at last count. Publishing is what they do best.

Congratulations! You've hired an expert to help you weed through all of those forms. Reward yourself with a relaxing drive through the country side

The Lazy Way

IF YOU'RE SO
INCLINED

To check out the whole enchilada, you can find a list of all current tax guides by calling 800-829-3676, or by contacting the IRS at their Web site (http://www.irs.ustreas.gov).

These include publication 17 ("Your Federal Income Tax"), designed for individual tax return preparation, and publication 334 ("Tax Guide for Small Businesses"), for small business owners.

If you don't have the time or energy to page through all those brochures, you can just pick up the phone and ask the IRS some questions yourself. However, you should know that while the IRS may wield a lot of power, they're not perfect (after all, they *are* the government). They make mistakes and they can steer you wrong when you call for advice.

If you call the IRS with a question, be sure to take notes while you're talking to the agent, so you can protect yourself if you get wrong information and you're audited. Be sure to include the date, the IRS employee's name, your questions, and the agent's answers. Keep those notes together with a copy of your completed return.

Even simpler than getting on the phone with an IRS agent is simply dialing up the IRS's prerecorded listing of answers to common tax questions. You can find specific information in 18 different categories—everything from tax credits, IRS notices, and electronic filing to IRS questions in Spanish—by dialing the IRS Teletax hotline at 800-829-4477. Touchtone service is available 24 hours a day, seven days a week; rotary service is available Monday through Friday from 7:30 a.m. to 5:30 p.m.

TELEFILING: PICK UP THAT PHONE!

For some people, the U.S. mail is just too much trouble. And who needs to spend time filling out all those forms? If you fit this profile, you can actually file your taxes without having to put pen to paper at all and get your refund within three weeks. It's possible with Telefile, an interactive computer system that automatically calculates your taxes and begins the electronic filing process over the phone.

This year, about 24 million single taxpayers received the special Telefile tax booklet. If you qualify, the government will automatically send you a special tax package explaining how the system works. Only those receiving a tax booklet who are single and have a touchtone phone can use Telefile. The government will send you a booklet about using the TeleFile system provided you:

- have no dependents
- made less than $50,000 last year
- file your return from the same address as last year

FILING ELECTRONICALLY

There are others of you out there who like the speed, safety, and ease of filing electronically but who don't fit the government's profile for Telefiling. These folks can still file electronically, but they must go through a tax preparer or an IRS-approved transmitter or company.

This method transmits your tax information over telephone lines directly to the IRS computer. You can file

QUICK n° PAINLESS

Telefile is completely paperless. If you owe tax, you can file early over the phone and pay by April 15.

whether you owe money or are due a refund (which usually arrives within 21 days). You also may have the convenience and safety of direct deposit of any refund check.

In many states, you can file your state tax return electronically along with the federal tax form; check with your tax preparer or transmitter. To find a professional who can file electronically for you, look in your local phone book or get a recommendation from a friend. Many companies also offer electronic filing as a benefit for employees; check with your employer.

COMPUTING TAXES THE EASY WAY

Those of you who are looking for a really zippy way to prepare your taxes, and who are reasonably competent with a computer, should check out the new tax preparation software. Programs such as the Kiplinger TaxCut, TurboTax, and MacInTax can be a real time-saver. And remember—when you buy the software, you can deduct the expense of the program!

For the busy person, this software can't be beat at organizing and streamlining your taxable details: You can use it all year to check on your ongoing tax liability, to plan your taxes, and so on. If you feel uncertain about accuracy after you prepare your return with a computer program, you can always hire a tax preparer to check it over later.

Last year, 8.2 million Americans filed their taxes through their computers. Using this software can reduce an 11-page conventional return to two pages. And

IF YOU'RE SO
INCLINED

You can also file electronically with a computer, tax software, and a modem; some online providers offer this service.

because you use an IRS-approved computer software program to compute your tax, there are fewer errors and faster processing of your return. Anyone who uses tax form 1040, 1040-A, or 1040EZ can participate.

If you are expecting a refund, you can opt for a check or direct deposit to your bank account, or have the refund applied to next year's estimated tax.

WHERE'S MY REFUND?

Okay. You've done the math, totaled the figures, licked the envelope, and beaten the deadline. How long will it take to get your refund? In the old days, you simply had to hang around your mailbox until that check arrived, two or three months later.

Surprise! Today there's a quick and easy way to find out, and it's as close as the nearest telephone. To find out the status of your tax refund, you can call the IRS Teletax hotline at 800-829-4477. Touchtone service is available 24 hours a day, seven days a week; rotary service is available Monday through Friday from 7:30 a.m. to 5:30 p.m. Make sure you have a copy of your return handy so you can answer the recorded questions.

You have back-to-back meetings till 9 p.m. You've got to pick up your daughter at day care, your son at Cub Scouts, and a box of plaster of Paris at the Piggly Wiggly for the school science fair. Who's got time to hang out at the mailbox checking for that refund and then running it to the bank when it finally shows up?

You'll be happy to know that for all you busy people out there, the government can deposit your refund

QUICK ⬤ PAINLESS

To prove that you got your return in on time, the IRS now will accept a receipt from approved private delivery services, such as Federal Express and United Parcel Service, in addition to a receipt from the U.S. Postal Service.

directly into any checking or savings bank account you choose—for free! You'll get your refund faster and there's no chance your check will get lost in the mail.

Interested? Fill in lines 60 b, c, and d on Form 1040.

HASSLE-FREE WAYS TO SORT OUT THOSE DEDUCTIONS

Once you've decided who's going to prepare your taxes—you, your computer, or your Uncle Bob the CPA—you get to the next part of the tax nightmare: adding up deductions.

Some people keep incredibly neat ledgers with tedious details about each and every tax-deductible purchase made during the entire year. Then there are the rest of us who have better things to do with our time all year than keep meticulous records about how much gas we used up when we drove to church to play the organ for the lady's auxiliary.

The easy way, the lazy way, to keep your records together is simply to throw them into one big drawer you've designated for that purpose. Each time you get a canceled check or a receipt for a deductible item, throw it in the drawer. It's a lot easier to search through one drawer than an entire house for every expense receipt when April 15 rolls around. Once you've located your potential Tax Receipt Drawer, you've got to figure out what counts as a tax-deductible item. How do you know what can be itemized? Start here:

- Taxes: state and local income taxes, real estate taxes, foreign taxes, personal property taxes

YOU'LL THANK YOURSELF LATER

To ensure your refund gets there early:

- **Mail your return early.**

- **Sign and date it properly.**

- **Use the address label that comes with your tax form.**

- **Don't forget to attach your W-2 form.**

- Interest expenses for home mortgages (there are limitations); points on purchasing a home

- Charitable contributions to tax-exempt organizations, both cash and property (within guidelines)

- Nonbusiness casualty and theft losses, such as storm damage to your home or theft of stereo equipment (amount must be more than 10 percent of adjusted gross income)

- Federal estate tax on IRA income; gambling losses up to gambling winnings; impairment-related work expenses of person with disabilities

Wait! There's more. . . . You can deduct these expenses if they total more than 2 percent of your adjusted gross income:

- Car expenses and other job-related business expenses (such as travel and entertaining)

- Educational expenses required by your employer to maintain or improve skills needed in your present job

- Professional dues, tools, and uniforms; legal expenses used to collect income; tax preparation fees; investment fees

- Cellular phone used for business

- Passport fee if the passport is for business travel

- Fees paid to your bank for a safe deposit box in which you keep taxable bonds or stock certificates

- Subscriptions to job-related magazines, and to newspapers and services that provide investment information or advice

IF YOU'RE SO
INCLINED

Save those receipts! Money spent on the job may be deductible—make sure you get your credit!

The cost of a home computer, if you can prove that the computer is required for your job

Now rein yourself in. There are still some things you can't deduct:

- political contributions
- homeowners association charges
- water bills (unless they are part of a business)
- estate, inheritance, legacy, or succession taxes
- credit card interest (except for a business)
- personal loan interest
- interest on loans where proceeds are used to purchase tax-exempt points if you are the seller of the property
- interest on a loan to buy open land (with no house)

Car expenses are an area that many folks add up for their taxes. Actual car expenses can include the cost of insurance, gas, oil, maintenance, repairs, car registration and licensing, and so on.

If you lease the car, you need to keep track of the lease payments. Actual expenses are prorated for the amount of business miles compared to total miles driven for the year. Thus, you need to read the mileage for the car on January 1 and then again on December 31. As with all deductions for mileage, use an odometer and keep meticulous records with dates and destinations.

MEDICAL EXPENSES: WHAT GOES WHERE?

Medical expenses are another area of potential deductions. You can deduct nonreimbursed medical expenses for yourself, your spouse, and dependents if the total is more than 7.5 percent of your adjusted gross income. This means that if your adjusted gross income is $50,000, you can start deducting medical expenses once you have spent more than $3,750.

Deductible expenses would include:

- Premiums on health insurance policies (including those for Medicare B and Medigap)

- Contact lenses and supplies

- Health insurance premiums paid for students, if the premiums are part of the tuition bill. Insurance costs must be included separately on the bill

- Driving devices for the handicapped

- Cost of cosmetic surgery *only* if required to correct a disfigurement caused by an accident or that was present at birth

- Childbirth classes

- Weight-loss and stop-smoking programs, if recommended by your doctor

- Remedial reading classes for a dyslexic child

- Travel to AA meetings, if they are recommended by your doctor

- Cost of senior citizen facilities if the patient is there specifically for medical treatment

A COMPLETE WASTE OF TIME

The 3 Worst Things to Do When Figuring Your Medical Expenses:

1. Don't keep the receipts.

2. Don't research what can and cannot be deducted.

3. Ignore them.

IF YOU'RE SO
INCLINED

If you've had to modify your home because of a medical condition, you also can qualify for a tax write-off, provided the costs (plus other unreimbursed medical expenses) exceed 7.5 percent of your adjusted gross income.

If you constructed a wheelchair ramp for your son's wheelchair, built a pool to exercise your bum knee, widened your door frames because your wife is in a wheelchair, or installed an air conditioner for your asthma, these could all be deducted. You can also deduct the electricity to run the air filtration system, or the paint to refurbish the wheelchair ramp.

Remember that if the work was done in December 1998 but you don't pay for it until January 1999, you can't deduct the expenses until you file your 1999 taxes, because it's when you actually pay for the work that counts. Moreover, if the improvement adds value to your home, you have to subtract that additional value from the deduction. You need an appraisal of your home before and after the improvement. If the modification boosts the value of your home, you can deduct only the amount by which the cost exceeded the increase in value. In other words, if a $5,000 air filtration system added $2,000 to the worth of your home, you can deduct only the $3,000 difference between the two.

On the other hand, some improvements required as a result of a medical condition may actually lower the value of your home. In that case, you can deduct the modification but *not* the decrease in value of the home. It may not seem fair, but the government writes the rules, and you've got to play by them.

Of course, the IRS didn't just fall off a potato truck. They realize that some folks who simply want a pool may try to weasel an unwarranted deduction by pretending there is a medical need for all that watery exercise. You'll need to verify your condition by having your doctor write a letter that says the modification is medically necessary.

You'll want to consult your tax adviser before making improvements, but here's an idea of what is deductible:

- entrance/exit ramps for wheelchairs
- door hardware
- areas in front of entrances and exits
- fire alarms and warning systems to accommodate the deaf or hearing impaired
- electrical outlets
- doorways/hallways
- bathrooms
- stairways
- handrails or grab bars
- lower kitchen cabinets
- wheelchair lifts (but not usually elevators)
- doctor-prescribed air filtration units or air conditioners

AUDITS THE EASY WAY

If there is one thing worse than having to sit down and do your taxes, it's having to sit down and explain to an IRS agent why you did your taxes the way you did. There is a lazy way to get through this if, despite your best efforts, you get an audit notice.

First, remember that the tax auditor is not necessarily a tax expert. Auditing is a stressful, often unpleasant job. Many auditors are young and inexperienced, and they may not know the subtle intricacies in the tax code.

YOU'LL THANK YOURSELF LATER

If you can't pay all the tax you owe, you should mail your return on time, pay what you can, and attach form 9465 outlining a monthly repayment plan. The IRS will contact you within 30 days to let you know if your plan has been approved.

You may well have the upper hand in the knowledge department, especially if you work with an experienced tax advisor—many of whom know more about taxes than the average IRS auditor.

Here's how to prepare to save time and energy:

- You need to document only those areas the audit notice mentions. If your audit doesn't mention checking into that trip to Tahiti you said was for business, ignore that part of your return.

- Get a CPA or enrolled agent to go with you. Bringing along expert help will cost you money, but it looks good and can save you time, stress—and maybe even more money.

- Gather all the documentation that you have for your return. Don't wait until the last minute to get your receipts in order.

- Make it as easy as possible for the auditor to review your materials. Be as organized as you can—don't dump your paperwork in a pile on his desk.

- Be polite. Your mother was right: You'll catch more flies with honey than with lemon juice.

Congratulations! You put it all together ahead of time! So spend Tax Day on a picnic with your loved ones!

The Lazy Way

Getting Time on Your Side

	The Old Way	**The Lazy Way**
Filing your return	2 hours	5 minutes
Finding out about your refund	2 months	5 minutes
Preparing your taxes	5 hours	30 minutes
Choosing a CPA	Weeks	2 days
Gathering receipts	Months	2 seconds
Stressing about April 14th	12 months	No time at all!

Chapter eleven

Making Insurance Intelligible

Insurance. It's a word that can strike terror into the hearts of time-pressed money managers. It takes time to study the different kinds of insurance, listen to insurance brokers, and select and write up the policies. But no matter how much you'd like to, you just can't avoid having some type of insurance—it's the price we pay for security in an insecure world.

If you own a home but your bank owns the mortgage, most likely they'll want you to have homeowner's insurance for their protection. The state wants you to have auto insurance in case you slam into somebody else's brand new Saab with your '57 Buick.

In addition to required insurance, you'll need to decide what coverage you need for your family, and at what cost. Riders, options, and basic insurance itself all come at a cost, so you need to review the price and the coverage as part of your total financial picture.

Is the situation hopeless? Not at all. Fortunately, there are some lazy ways to approach insurance.

PHONE IN YOUR POLICY

Just as telecommuting is the wave of the future, more and more companies are making it possible for you to arrange for insurance over the phone. Through Travellers' Insurance, you can arrange for car, life, and disability assurance policies over the phone, without ever getting up off the sofa.

PAYING WITH PLASTIC

Those of you who don't like the trouble of writing out a check to pay for your insurance may be pleased to know that many companies are now allowing you to charge premiums on a major credit card.

The positive side to this is that you save the time and effort of writing out the check. The down side is that you're paying for insurance on credit, which means that you're adding high interest charges to your insurance bill.

AUTOMATIC DEDUCTION

Many companies allow you to pay for different types of insurance through automatic deductions at work. If you have this opportunity, take advantage of it! It beats having to write the checks, lick the stamps, and remember to mail the payments on time.

BE YOUR OWN INSURANCE AGENT

Then there's the hassle of signing up with an insurance policy in the first place. While some insurance is absolutely vital, you may be able to provide your own insurance for many types of risk by putting the funds aside on your own, such as money to pay dental bills, for a nursing home stay, and so on. An added benefit is that if you put the funds in a money market account, a CD, or even a savings account, you're earning interest.

REVIEW YOUR POLICY

The best place to start looking at your insurance coverage, of course, is at work, by reviewing the benefits provided by your employer. It's important when you start a new job that you understand both the salary and benefits. Disability, health, and life insurance are often provided, and should be a base from which you build your coverage.

JUST HOW DOES MY COMPANY RATE, ANYWAY?

You don't want to buy insurance from a company that's going to go belly up in a year. Take a little time up front to make sure you'll have coverage when you need it by checking out the company's ratings.

Insurance companies are rated by five services: A.M. Best & Co., Duff & Phelps, Standard & Poor's, Moody's, and the newest—Weiss Research. *Consumer Reports,*

QUICK n' PAINLESS

When choosing an insurance agent, look for one designated both as a CLU (certified life underwriter) and a ChFC (chartered financial consultant). These initials are the sign of education and ethics.

Financial World, and other financial magazines usually offer an annual listing of the top-rated companies, and you can find online guidance, too. (Some companies are tougher raters than others: Weiss is tough, while A.M. Best gives more high grades.) Two or three credit ratings will give you a good idea of how sound your company is. You can get the current rating information for free from your agent; review the material and check on the company yourself. Buying an insurance policy is an investment. Take the same amount of time for this that you do for your other investments.

What you want to do is to buy coverage to protect yourself against a broad range of risk, with enough protection to insure what you can't afford to cover yourself. Two life insurance companies with particularly low rates are USAA Life (800-531-8000) and Veritas (800-552-3553).

When you're buying insurance, don't overestimate your risk and buy too much of the wrong kind of coverage.

What's the wrong kind?

In addition, don't bother insuring yourself against losses that wouldn't be catastrophic for you. In general, if the policy doesn't cost much, it doesn't cover much. Here are a few to avoid:

- extended warranties

- dental insurance (Unless your employer throws this one in for free, it's not a good investment. Dental coverage usually includes only a few teeth cleanings a year and severely limits the expensive stuff.)

- package insurance (This doesn't cost much, but in general the U.S. postal system rarely loses or damages things.)
- contact lens insurance (You can buy contact lenses through the mail for less than the cost of this insurance.)
- credit card insurance (Buying a special policy to pay off your credit card debt if you die is extremely expensive, because the benefit is so small. A good life insurance policy is a better bet.)

HOW MUCH IS ENOUGH?

You can spend hours figuring out exactly how much life insurance you think you're going to need, or you can compute it the quick way: Simply multiply your annual income by five. If you make $100,000, you'll need $500,000 in life insurance to protect your family.

MORTGAGE INSURANCE: WHOM DOES IT REALLY BENEFIT?

Insurance is important if you or your partner dies prematurely, particularly if you are buying a home based on two incomes. You should definitely have enough life insurance (for both spouses) to cover the mortgage. However, where you buy the insurance is another matter—and the bank's policy is probably not your best choice.

Mortgage insurance is what is known as "decreasing term insurance." You start with a monthly payment based on the initial mortgage amount, but the premiums

IF YOU'RE SO
INCLINED

To learn more about insurance from the American Association of Individual Investors, point your online browser here:

http://www.aaii.org/insuranc/insurancindex.html

If you move often, buy an insurance policy separate from the mortgage so you can "carry" the coverage with you to your next home.

never decrease as you pay off your mortgage. Thus, if you have an $85,000 mortgage and you die during the year you bought the home, the policy will pay off the full mortgage. But if you die in the thirteenth year of the mortgage, the death benefits cover only the amount needed to cover the payoff, which might be only $40,000.

This insurance might make sense if you have some reason to believe you or your spouse may not live long and would not be able to pass the medical exam required by traditional insurance.

INSURING THE KIDS

A life insurance policy for your child isn't the best way to invest your money, but it can provide a death benefit, cash value growth, and future insurability. A policy on your child is the easy way to get the child to save. It can also avoid hassles if your child develops a health problem that would interfere with her ability to buy life insurance for herself when she's older. Your children will always have the benefits of any policies you have purchased for them.

Remember, of course, that the policy is not the total investment package for children; there are other investments that can earn more money. Grandparents may find that a life insurance policy on a child is a wonderful gift to provide some cash value during the child's lifetime and for retirement.

HEALTH INSURANCE

Most folks don't realize it, but they have a medical information report that is very similar to a credit report—and "bad" things on it can be a real pain. Whenever you try to get health or life insurance, you can bet the companies are consulting this report. There can be mistakes on the report, and you have a right to see it. If you find a mistake, you have the right to request a correction—but the burden is yours to prove the file wrong. You may need to contact doctors you've seen before to correct the problem.

When it comes to health insurance, the easiest and most sensible way to be protected is to buy a good general policy. Specific health insurance policies aren't necessary if you have a good policy that covers you for any and all illnesses.

Specific health insurance policies (such as a "cancer" policy) often have so many restrictions that even if you get the disease you insured yourself against, it won't pay for most of the things you need.

MEDICARE

Medicare, Part A, is mandatory health insurance that covers people 65 years of age or older, anyone who is on Social Security disability, or anyone who is undergoing kidney dialysis treatment. When you sign up for Social Security, you automatically sign up for Medicare, Part A, which covers hospitalization costs, some skilled nursing care, and home health care. When you're signing up for

QUICK **n** PAINLESS

To get a copy of your medical information report, write to the Medical Information Bureau at P.O. Box 105, Essex Station, Boston, MA 02112, or call 617-426-3660.

Part A, you should think strongly about adding Part B coverage at the same time—it's a lot easier this way.

Part B is a supplement to Medicare, Part A (the present rate is $43.80 per month, but it is always increasing). Part B covers physician's services, certain laboratory expenses, and so on. When you sign up for Medicare, you are asked if you want Part B. If you don't take Part B when you enroll for Medicare, Part A, you are surcharged at a 10-percent-per-year penalty when you do sign up for the coverage. This means that if you don't take the coverage at age 65 and then decide at 70 you do want coverage, the premiums will be 50 percent higher than if you had acquired the coverage at age 65. So think hard before declining part B!

If you're worried at all about paying for your health care while you're on Medicare, also think about getting a Medicare supplement policy (called "Medigap"), which is designed to cover the things Medicare doesn't. There are so many of these plans available that choosing one can be difficult. To make it easier on consumers, all states (except Minnesota, Massachusetts, and Wisconsin) limit the number of these Medigap plans to 10 standard versions, designated "A" through "J." Plan A has the most basic coverage; plan J has the most extensive coverage. All of these plans cover specific medical areas that aren't covered (or are only partially covered) under Medicare.

SOCIAL SECURITY: CHECK IT OUT

We're all hoping that Social Security will be there when we retire. None of us know for sure, but there's an easy

IF YOU'RE SO
INCLINED

For help with Medicare or Medigap, call Apprise (800-783-7067). It's a free government service, which is offered through your local Agency on Aging.

way to find out what your benefits would be when you retire. Contact the Social Security Administration at (800) 772-1213, and ask for an Earnings and Benefit Estimate Statement for your account (Form SSA-7004-SM).

This statement gives a record of your earnings and can provide you with an idea of your monthly payment at normal retirement age. For people born before 1960, that's age 65. For people born after 1960, it's 67.

CAR INSURANCE

If you drive a car, you need car insurance. But you'll be happy to know there are some easy ways to save money on these policies. Here's how:

- Raise your deductibles. You aren't likely to file many claims, so there's no need to pay lots of money in extra yearly premiums.

- Drop collision and/or comprehensive coverage on older cars (or those worth less than $4,000).

- Insist on discounts for insuring your car and home with the same company.

- Increase collision and comprehensive deductibles on newer cars.

- Comparison shop (prices for the same coverage can vary by hundreds of dollars from one company to the next). You can do this online to save time.

- Take advantage of low-mileage discounts.

- Take advantage of automatic seat belt or air bag discounts.

YOU'LL THANK YOURSELF LATER

Some luxury cars cost a lot more to insure than most other cars. For an easy way to check out how much more, write to the Insurance Institute for Highway Safety, 1005 Glebe Road, Arlington, VA 22201, and request their Highway Loss Data Chart.

■ Ask about other discounts (such as discounts for no tickets, insuring more than one car, no accidents in three years, drivers over age 50, driver training courses, anti-theft devices, anti-lock brakes, good grades for students, college students away from home without a car, and so on).

Another easy way to save money with your car is to decline insurance coverage when renting, if your personal car insurance provides coverage while driving a rental car. But one caveat: If you don't have comprehensive or collision insurance on your auto policy, you won't have it on the rental car either without extra (or credit card) coverage, either.

HOMEOWNER'S INSURANCE

If you don't have the time or energy to carry all sorts of insurance, some of you still should carry extra liability coverage, known as a PCAT (personal catastrophic) policy, if you:

■ have a swimming pool

■ own an aggressive dog

■ are wealthy

If someone is injured on your property, will $300,000 coverage be enough if it is known you are wealthy and have assets that can be taken in a lawsuit? Personal umbrella coverage is available at very reasonable prices. It covers not just accidents that might happen at home, but catastrophic car accidents. If, for example, your car

QUICK ■ PAINLESS

For those who live in a high crime area and can't get homeowner's insurance, contact the federal government's Home Insurance Program to help you in this situation. For more information, call 800-638-8780.

went out of control and plunged into five others, the damages might well exceed coverage provided by regular auto insurance. An umbrella policy would cover this.

You should verify that the umbrella coverage is supplemental to your homeowners' coverage. Also note that some companies' general liability policies don't provide supplemental auto liability coverage.

Those of you who don't pay too much attention to your homeowner's insurance premium notices when they come for payment might want to think about getting an inflation rider on the policy. Inflation riders automatically increase the amount of coverage you have as the cost of replacement increases. They take the responsibility for your home insurance coverage off your shoulders. If you don't have this coverage, you have to compare the value of your home with your coverage every few years.

The problem with an inflation rider is that you may be overinsuring your property. In one recent case, a family insured their home for twice its value, mistakenly thinking that if the property was damaged, they would receive the insured value rather than the replacement cost.

DISABILITY: YOU MIGHT WANT TO TAKE ANOTHER LOOK

Lots of people out there who don't have time and money to waste sidestep disability insurance, figuring that if they are disabled they'll automatically be covered by Social Security disability. Wrong! Seventy percent of all applicants for Social Security disability are turned down.

YOU'LL THANK YOURSELF LATER

You won't pay taxes on disability income if you pay for your disability insurance yourself. If your employer pays for your disability, then you do have to pay tax on the benefits—so you need more benefits.

Yet you have a better chance of being disabled before age 65 than dying before that age, so you'd better listen up. Social Security disability applies only if you become "severely" disabled and can't work before reaching retirement age. Note that the inability to work doesn't mean the inability to handle your current job—it means the inability to perform *any* job. Thus, if you're a surgeon and you can't operate, you wouldn't qualify for Social Security disability if you could still do office work.

Also, remember that Social Security disability is based only on what your monthly Social Security benefit would have been. It has nothing to do with your current salary. Disability insurance is imperative if your family depends on your income to live, to maintain their current station in life, to pay for a home, and so on. Remember that health insurance pays only your medical bills; it won't cover your lost salary. Most disability policies pay 60 percent of your salary.

Disability insurance can be confusing. Here are a few things to look for:

- **Definition of disability.** An "own-occupation" policy pays benefits if you can't perform the work you usually do. Other policies pay only if you can't do the job for which you are "reasonably trained." Own-occupation policies are the most expensive, because it's more likely that the insurer will have to pay you. It may not be worth the extra cost unless you're in a high-income specialized job and would have to take a big pay cut in switching jobs.

IF YOU'RE SO
INCLINED

For information on purchasing disability insurance on your own, check with:

- USAA (800-531-8000)
- Wholesale Insurance Network (800-808-5810)
- Direct Insurance Services (800-622-3699)

- **Guaranteed renewable.** This guarantees that your policy can't be canceled if you get sick. If you get a policy that requires you to take physicals every so often, you could lose your coverage when you need it.

- **Waiting period.** This is the period of time between when you became disabled and when the plan starts paying. You should take the longest waiting period you can, since the longer the waiting period, the cheaper the policy. The minimum on most policies is 30 days, and the maximum can be up to two years. A good average to shoot for is 90 days or 6 months.

- **Cost-of-living adjustments.** These automatically boost your benefits either by a set amount or in concert with inflation.

- **Future insurability.** This clause lets you buy additional coverage later on, but it's usually not necessary unless you're making much less today than you expect to earn in the future.

A COMPLETE WASTE OF TIME

The 3 Worst Things to Do About Your Insurance:

1. Don't get any.
2. Get too much.
3. Pay too much.

Getting Time on Your Side

	The Old Way	The Lazy Way
Buying an insurance policy	2 hours	10 minutes
Making payments	15 minutes	5 minutes
Compare companies	2 hours	15 minutes
Choosing an agent	Weeks	A few days
Choosing a policy	2 hours	30 minutes
Obtaining information reports	2 weeks	5 minutes

Chapter
twelve

It's Child's Play—
Kids and Money

As any parent who has ever dragged a child past Toys 'R' Us knows, teaching your children how to spend money isn't hard—teaching them how to spend money carefully and with intelligence is the real challenge. Before kids are able to grasp the concept of "cost," they are on intimate terms with the idea of "want." Learning that fulfilling "want" costs money can be a rude awakening.

Whether you have a lot or a little, money can influence your moods, relationships, personality, goals, and dreams. Teaching your children how to handle money—how to respect its potential without worshipping its power—is a wonderful gift. Teaching them early how to handle money through earning, saving, and smart spending is giving them the tools to navigate through life as mature, responsible adults.

So how can you educate them about money matters when you can't even get them to clean their rooms? Fortunately, there are lots of strategies and tips that can make the job

much easier. There really is a lazy way to help your kids learn how to handle money.

ALLOWANCES: YES OR NO?

The earlier you start teaching kids about money, the easier it will be. The easiest way to get started—it hardly takes a moment—is to give them an allowance around age 5 or 6, when they're old enough to understand that Mommy and Daddy go to the store and buy things with money. The fact is, kids can't learn how to manage money if they never have any, or if they live on sporadic handouts. For this reason, establishing an allowance is the smart way to start kids off down that road to financial stability.

Experts agree that an allowance is a good idea. What they don't agree on is just how to handle that allowance. Do you tie it to chores, or do you give money with no strings attached? Is $1 a week too little? Is $10 too much?

The important thing is to give kids enough money that they have something to manage. It's pretty hard to save and invest a portion of your allowance and spend the rest if you only get a quarter a week.

One good plan is to divide your child's allowance into four parts, including money for long-term investments, an amount for short-term goals (such as a computer game or video), a no-strings allowance, and an amount to donate to a charity of the child's choice. This method reinforces the importance of saving for both the short and long term while still providing the freedom to "blow" a small amount of money. Most valuable—and something that parents often overlook—it reinforces the importance of giving a portion of the child's income to charity.

Allowances can be enough to give even the most energetic parents a headache. You can get all caught up in the details if you let yourself. Instead, concentrate on the simple facts first: Give your kids a little money to manage, and see how it goes. Don't obsess about the details.

So sit down in your Barcalounger, put your feet up, and read some simple tips from money experts to get you started the easy way:

- Start each child out with 50 cents or a dollar a week.

- Give change, if possible, so the child can more easily divide the money and have some to spend and some to save.

- On shopping trips, show children what they can buy with one week's allowance and what they can buy if they save their money for a few weeks.

- Don't tie chores to allowance—that way, you avoid monumental hassles. Chores are the price you pay for being in a family. An allowance is a learning tool to help kids handle money.

BANK ON IT

Giving kids an allowance is an easy way to start teaching them about saving. If things seem to be proceeding fairly smoothly, you're ready for the next step: organized financing.

You'll be happy to know that many banks offer programs for children to start them out—you don't even

QUICK n' PAINLESS

Board games can get kids interested in money. Try:

- Monopoly
- Payday
- The Allowance Game
- The Game of Life

YOU'LL THANK YOURSELF LATER

For information about credit cards and checking accounts for kids, write Young Americans Bank at 311 Steele Street, Denver, CO 80206; call 303-321-2265 (or 303-321-BANK); or visit their Web site at http://www.theyoungamericans.org.

have to lift a finger! But if your bank doesn't have a specific program for children, you can take them on an initial visit sometime around age 5 and with two goals in mind: to show them the bank and familiarize them with the surroundings and to open that first savings account.

If you haven't already done so, open a savings account today. This is a simple, no-stress practice that gets kids in the swing of the saving idea. Most local banks will open children's accounts with as little as $1 to $25. The same is true for credit unions; some even waive minimum balance requirements.

Of course, many parents and grandparents open savings accounts in a child's name at birth. They use it to deposit gifts of money for the child or build a nest egg for the child's future. But what if children don't know what to do with the money when they're old enough to use it?

This is where your job comes in. It's not that hard, it doesn't take up much time and energy—with a little thought and preparation, you can lay the groundwork for a lifetime of responsible living.

Next, make sure your child knows how to write a check. If you can't find a local bank to issue a checking account to a child, you can get one from Young Americans Bank in Denver, Colorado, "the world's first (and only) bank just for young people." Young Americans Bank offers checking and savings accounts, credit cards, and small business loans, and provides extensive financial counseling and education.

As the only bank in the world that caters to kids, Young Americans has customers in all 50 states and in 12 foreign countries. Kids can open accounts through the mail, sign and send in their signature cards, and send in deposits. All customers under age 18 need an adult to cosign for loans, credit cards, and accounts.

On average, the bank suggests 12 as a good age for a credit card or a checking account. Bankers spend a lot of time counseling potential customers. Because education is their focus, they want to make sure that children fully understand their financial obligations.

The bank also offers loans (with an adult cosigner required) to finance small businesses. Youngsters fill out a full loan application and create their own business plan first.

SAVE FOR AMERICA: SCHOOL PROGRAMS GET INTO THE ACT

There are other ways to teach kids about saving. The "Save For America" program is a computerized school savings program that teaches elementary students how to maintain a savings account. Schools must be sponsored by a bank in order to utilize the Save For America computer software. Save For America is the only school savings program for elementary students that has been approved by the U.S. Department of Education. It has 142 bank sponsors and over 3,500 schools participating in its national savings program. For more information, call 206-746-0331.

A COMPLETE WASTE OF TIME

The 3 Worst Things to Do When It Comes to Saving for College:

1. Don't start saving.

2. Don't look at scholarships and grants.

3. Don't get your kids in on the act.

KIDS AND CREDIT

Now that you've started off with checking and savings accounts, you come to the next financial opportunity: credit. Should kids have their own credit card?

According to the law, they can't—not until they reach the age of majority (that's 18 or 21, depending on your state). (The Young Americans Bank offers credit cards to kids if a parent cosigns the application.)

Of course, you can always hand over your credit card to your kids—but beware. In the eyes of the law, if your child takes your credit card and goes wild, the fact that she had it in her possession is considered to be authorization enough. If your child has your card, a store has the reasonable belief that it can approve almost any charges.

Of course, if your child took the card without your knowledge, you could take advantage of federal regulations limiting your liability to no more than $50 in charges. But you would have to notify the issuer that the card had been stolen, which could lead to a criminal investigation of your child.

MUTUAL FUNDS

Once your kids are comfortable with checking and savings accounts, you're ready to move from saving to investing. Probably the best and the easiest way to start is by opening a kid-oriented mutual fund, paid for with an automatic bank account deduction—no muss, no fuss, no checks to write, no frantic phone calls to your broker when the market dithers. Once you set up the account, it hums along on its own quite nicely.

Those of you who worry about what would happen if several thousand dollars suddenly fell into your child's lap do have an alternative: Twentieth Century's Giftrust Investors (800-345-2021). This is an older, more aggressive growth fund that can be given only as a gift to a child. The gift is placed in an irrevocable trust for any period you specify, as long as it's at least 10 years. (The most popular time period is 18 years, probably because that's the age kids head off to college.)

Every year, the child receives a statement listing the account's value, along with a personal message, such as "To Kara from Mom & Dad." The minimum investment is $500; the fund's average annual return rate over 10 years has been 26.9 percent.

Many other well-known no-load (no-fee) funds will lower minimum investment requirements (usually ranging from $1,000 to $2,500) for Uniform Gift To Minor Accounts (also called custodial accounts). The Vanguard Group (800-662-2739), for example, lowers its minimum from $3,000 to $1,000. T. Rowe Price (800-638-5660) cuts its $2,500 minimum to $1,000 for a UGMA.

KID-APPEALING INDIVIDUAL STOCKS

Although mutual funds are a more diversified investment gift and require just about no maintenance, some kids relate better to an individual stock, something they can hold in their hands, especially if it's stock in a company that produces things they're interested in. Here are some stocks kids may find interesting:

QUICK ⬤ PAINLESS

Not sure about investing? If you had put $1,000 in Twentieth Century's Giftrust Investors back in 1983 and never added a penny, the account would have been worth $6,600 in 1993.

If you buy less than 100 shares of a stock, use a discount broker such as Muriel Siebert, Charles Schwab, or Quick & Reilly. Alternatively, for stocks at less than $100 per share, A.G. Edwards (314-289-3000) charges just 16 percent of the stock's price.

- Coca-Cola
- Disney
- Hershey
- Kellogg
- McDonald's
- Microsoft
- NIKE
- Pepsi
- Reebok
- Sara Lee
- Toys 'R' Us

A handful of companies throw in extra goodies for stockholders, to attract and keep investors. These can make great gifts for kids, and what could be simpler than picking up the phone and ordering some?

Tandy Corp.: This Fort Worth–based electronics firm offers shareholders a 10-percent discount from time to time (usually at Christmas and Hanukkah) on purchases up to $10,000 at its Radio Shack stores. Call 817-390-3700 for details.

General Mills: For years this Minneapolis conglomerate has offered shareholders a holiday gift box with samples of its products and a Betty Crocker cookbook for $21.95 each (but valued at twice that much). If you own stock, you can also send up to nine packages to those on your holiday list. For order forms, call 612-540-2444.

- **Anheuser-Busch:** Shareholders of this St. Louis company get a 25 percent discount on items in the company's catalog, and a 15 percent discount on admission each year to its theme parks, including Sea World and Busch Gardens. For more information, call 314-577-2000.

- **Wrigley:** This Chicago gum company sends a box of 20 packs of gum to shareholders every December. For more information, call 312-644-2121.

- **Walt Disney:** With this stock, you can purchase a gold card membership for $50 ($15 off the regular price) that entitles you to all kinds of discounts at Disney attractions throughout the country. For more information, call 818-560-1000.

EE SAVINGS BONDS

Many Americans still get queasy when thinking about taking the stock market plunge. If you're one of them, and you're looking for a simple, easy, and no-fail investment for kids, you'll find EE Savings Bonds reassuring. They sell for as little as $25, they're easy to find, and they don't incur state or federal taxes if used to pay for college tuition (income restrictions do apply here). Give your local bank a call about buying savings bonds without a commission or fee.

Savings bonds are one of the easiest investments available. The interest rates won't knock your socks off, but if the stock market takes a plunge, you won't lose your shirt, either.

IF YOU'RE SO
INCLINED

For the budding business executive over age 10, check out BUSINESS KIT (305-445-8869), a briefcase filled with everything a kid needs to know about starting up, managing, and running a business. It comes with a newsletter and one-year membership in the Business Kids Club.

A COMPLETE WASTE OF TIME

The 3 Worst Things to Do with Kids and Money:

1. Punish them by taking their allowance away so they end up never having any money to spend.

2. Give kids everything they want. You had a hard life, and you don't want them to suffer!

3. Teach by your bad example: You don't save, so why should they?

IRAS: NOT JUST FOR OLD FOLKS ANYMORE

We've all heard our accountants lecturing us about the tax benefits of investing in IRAs. But did you know that kids can invest as well, as long as they are working and earning an income? It's fast, it's effortless, and it makes good economic sense.

If your children are pulling in money from summer jobs, it's a good time to look at how you can encourage saving through IRAs. If you invest $2,000 in an IRA that earns 8 percent a year when you're 30, it will grow to $29,571 by the time you're 65. That's not bad!

Now imagine how much you'd have if you'd started investing your salary back when you were a 15-year-old soda jerk. In 50 years, $2,000 would grow—are you ready?—to $93,803. What could be simpler than that? Invest and forget!

Unfortunately, under the current rules, it's pretty hard for a baby to open an IRA, unless she started raking in money as a baby model or an infant TV star. That's because IRA contributions have to come from earned income. Doting parents or grandparents can't open an IRA for little Junior, nor can IRAs be funded from inheritances, income from trusts, or investments in the child's name.

However, if your child works in the summer or after school, she could easily earn enough to make a significant IRA contribution. The rules allow an individual to put up to 100 percent of earned income into an IRA.

Of course, those of you with kids know it might be hard to induce them to part with $2,000 that they could be blowing on Metallica tapes and tattoos. Here's the simple solution: You can't put your own money into your child's IRA, but you can replace money that your child invests. If your daughter earns $2,000 waiting tables at Big Boy over the summer, she can put it all into an IRA. You can then write her a check for $2,000. She gets to keep her income, and you can sleep nights knowing that she's on her way to a comfortable retirement.

Now here comes the fun part. Let's say your son earned at least $2,000 a year since age 15, and you helped him put $2,000 a year into IRAs for seven years (until he earned enough to do it on his own). That $14,000 contribution would grow to $527,444 by the time he reached 65, assuming an 8-percent return!

Of course, many parents may not be able to spare $2,000, especially if they're already struggling to salt away college money. But remember that anything is better than nothing, and smaller amounts would grow at the same pace.

Teaching children to be lifelong savers is important. When they are young adults, they may need to rely on the money they invested throughout their lives. By saving today, they will have the money they need to go to college, buy a car, start a business, deal with emergencies, and plan for retirement. Understanding money and saving gives children the freedom they need to make important decisions about their future.

Congratulations! You've gotten your kid to start putting money aside in an account. Go pour yourself some lemonade and take a nap in the hammock. You've earned it!

The Lazy Way

Getting Time on Your Side

	The Old Way	The Lazy Way
Investing money	1 hour	2 minutes
Saving for college	1 hour	2 minutes
Managing allowance	30 minutes	5 minutes
Opening an account	2 hours	20 minutes
Choosing a stock	1 hour	10 minutes
Creating a credit history	2 hours	10 minutes

Real News on Real Estate

Even thinking about buying or selling a home gives most people a headache. Who's got time to deal with realtors, home inspectors, pest companies, mortgage brokers, title searchers, and the rest of the flotsam and jetsam that comes along with the real estate industry?

Americans have always been under the impression that it's better to own than rent, which is all well and good unless you're the poor sap who has to sell your house or buy a new one. Still, you'll be happy to know there are shortcuts for those busy folks out there without the time to fuss with all the particulars.

THE BEST TIME TO SELL—FROM THE OUTSIDE

Let's say you're ready to sell your house. The best time to plant that "for sale" sign in your lawn is generally in the spring—although this can vary depending on which part of

The easiest trick to make your house look good is to repaint the front door.

the country you live in. For example, college towns and areas near medical centers have unique timetables, depending on when the next group of students arrives (September) or the next batch of health professionals moves in to begin their contracts (July 1).

Even so, the most popular time for most areas is still the spring, when folks come popping out of their houses after a long winter anxious for a new, fresh start in a new, fresh house. Spring is the time when most houses look their best, too. The lawn hasn't yet been eaten up with crabgrass or been burned brown by the midsummer sun. Cherry, apple, and pear trees are blooming, and spring flowers are popping up everywhere.

Many homes are bought at this time by people who weren't particularly thinking about moving—they just saw a sign while riding by. What could be simpler than selling your house this way?

HASSLE-FREE WAYS TO CATCH THOSE EASY BUYERS

To snag those effortless buyers, you'll need to have a house that looks good as prospective purchasers are walking, riding, or skating through your neighborhood. You'll be happy to know you can spruce up the outside of your house without a lot of effort, and without sinking buckets of money into it that you won't be able to get out at settlement time.

Here are a few easy things that the laziest of home-owners can do:

- Make certain the landscaping looks good. If you don't have time (and who does?), hire a couple of neighborhood kids to clean away old leaves under bushes, weed the flower beds, and put down new mulch.

- While they're at it, have them hack away those old shrubs to let light into the house.

- Spend a few dollars at your local greenhouse and buy some flowers for window boxes and beds around the foundation. This doesn't cost much, it's not hard to plunk a few plants into the ground, and even if you don't have time to take care of them, they'll probably survive long enough to attract a few months' worth of potential house buyers.

- Don't leave kids' toys, old dog bones, or last week's newspaper circulars littering the lawn.

FIX-IT EXPRESS: WHAT TO FIX AND WHAT TO LEAVE ALONE

Of course, eventually those prospective buyers cruising by the outside of your house will want to take a peek indoors, too. Interestingly, most realtors say that the final decision to buy a particular property is most often decided by the wife. That's why many builders have designed homes with this in mind, spending lots of extra money on fancy kitchens and big closets. If you want to sell your house easily, take a hint from those who know and think about what might attract a woman to your house. If you are a woman, imagine what you'd be looking for in a

IF YOU'RE SO
INCLINED

When you're showing your home, simmer some cinnamon, cloves, and nutmeg in a pot of water on the stove. The aroma makes your kitchen seem homey!

home. If you're a man, ask your wife, your mom, your sister, or a woman friend what she thinks is a must-have.

You'll be happy to hear that large fix-up expenses shouldn't be necessary; too many homeowners over-improve their properties and then can't get the money back out when they sell. Besides, major improvements take a lot of time and effort. Never make your home the largest building in the neighborhood—leave that to the Joneses.

So what are some fast 'n' easy ways to spruce up your house so it looks saleable? Here's what you should concentrate on:

- Repaint indoors with light, neutral colors. Go for shades that would work with most types of furniture.

- Clean your carpets, but don't replace them. The new owners will probably put in their own, anyway.

- Clean furniture and rooms thoroughly.

- Straighten out the attic and basement.

- Remove some furniture to make the rooms look larger.

If you're determined to spend some money on your house before you sell, then invest it in your kitchen. Install central air if you want to make a big investment. Fix that broken tile in the kitchen and replace that cracked mirror in the bathroom. You can usually recoup the money you spend to fix a cracked driveway, repaint peeling exteriors and walls, and mend a leaky roof.

A COMPLETE WASTE OF TIME

The 3 Worst Things to Do When Selling Your House:

1. Add a swimming pool.

2. Build a deck.

3. Put in a new fireplace.

Having things in good repair sends a message to prospective buyers that you're the sort of homeowner who cares. When people notice problems with things they can see in your house, they start wondering if the things they can't see are in bad shape, too.

Of course, there are some things you'll really have to fix. If you've got radon gas floating around in your basement, or a tainted well in your back yard, you'll have to prove that you've taken care of these issues. Most municipalities have certain rules when it comes to home selling. Some require that particular safety issues be addressed, such as with pest checks and handrails on stairways. Taking care of these now will save time and money later.

HOME WARRANTIES

Nervous first-time home buyers are often scared about taking the plunge into home ownership in case something major goes wrong in the first several years. The simplest and easiest way to deal with this is to buy home warranty coverage, which (after a small deductible) will fix any problems the buyer runs into. You can get a good general home warranty policy for about $225; the more you pay, the more coverage you can get.

REAL MEN USE REAL ESTATE AGENTS

If you really want to sell your home with the least amount of muss and fuss, you'll run, not walk, to the nearest realtor's office. There's no law that says you've

Make sure that you've checked out all of your options before deciding on which agent to use—and make sure you get references!

got to use an agent—you can certainly paint your own "for sale" sign, run your own ads, and spend every waking moment opening your own cupboard doors to perfect strangers.

The lazy way to selling a home almost requires you to turn the real estate reins over to the professionals. A real estate agent can quite often get you more money for your home than you would get on your own, with a lot less effort. Realtors know the market and have the clientele, and they can tell whether that sweet old couple in the 1924 Studebaker really can afford your place or not. You pay for their expert advice, and you save a lot of time.

In the litigious world we live in, if you aren't using a realtor you should work closely with a real estate attorney to guarantee you have followed all the rules as required by law.

When you're looking for a real estate agent, you'll want a person with experience and integrity. When you're ready to sell your home, interview three prospective realtors who were recommended to you, and ask for references.

DISCOUNT BROKERS: NOT ALL THEY'RE CRACKED UP TO BE

You may want to stay away from a discount broker, however, if you don't have lots of time. Discount brokers charge less than the standard real estate commission in your area, and since you get what you pay for, this means that a great deal of the burden of selling your house will fall on your shoulders—as well as the liability and responsibility. Using a discount broker is possible, but it takes up an awful lot of time; you need to do your homework and seek competent advice.

"FOR SALE BY OWNER" COMPANIES

Another time-saving alternative is a "For Sale by Owner" real estate company. These companies are set up to help you through the process of selling your home. They are not your agent; they serve as advisors. You pay an up-front fee (anywhere from $700 to $1,000) and get a menu of items they can handle, each with a fee. It's often an easier way to sell a home than by going through a regular real estate agent, but you must be careful, because you can end up paying the same or even more than you would with a full-service broker.

SELLING THE EASY WAY

If you want to sell your house the easy way, be sure to walk out the back door when potential buyers are walking in the front. It's important for prospective buyers to be able to discuss their misgivings about your hideous taste in wallpaper, or the funny bump in the wall that doesn't seem quite right to them. It's not likely they'll be so forthcoming if you're standing there in the corner hanging on every word. Realtors need to know buyers' objections so they can attempt to neutralize them, and they need the information to discover the type of home the buyers want.

A COMPLETE WASTE OF TIME

The 3 Worst Things to Do When Selling Your Home:

1. Try and do it all yourself.

2. Pay too much for an under-qualified agent.

3. Don't do your homework on selling a home in your area.

BUYING THE EASY WAY

Unless you've decided to move in with your children or to rent, when you sell your home you're going to need to buy another one to move into.

If you're thinking about making an offer on a piece of real estate, you should have the property reviewed by an inspector. You'll be able to find out whether that lake in the attic is serious, whether the furnace is likely to implode during the first cold snap, and what sort of creatures are living underneath the porch. Although everything is negotiable, most inspections are paid for by the buyer.

MORTGAGES 'R' US

When it comes to shopping for a mortgage, you'll probably have an easier time with a local lender than with a bank conglomerate the size of a small Eastern bloc country. Dealing locally means your banker may even know you by name—always a plus when negotiating a loan. If you have to, you can hand-deliver payments when they're due. When you are mailing to a post office box in another state, you have no control over when they credit the payment, which can subject you to late fees. Also, it's nice to be able to call locally if there are problems with your loan.

And there are likely to be problems with your loan. The bank may lose copies of your application. They'll forget to mention certain fees. Or perhaps they won't be able to find proof that you paid off your last loan. The person who has never had a problem while getting a mortgage is the person whose father is president of the bank.

BROKERING A MORTGAGE

If you anticipate any problems in obtaining a mortgage—there was that little matter of an unpaid piano bill four years ago—or if you've already been denied, you might want to visit a mortgage broker before passing go and collecting $200. A mortgage broker is a person whose job is to match you with a lender.

When it comes to mortgages, it pays to shop around. This does not mean you have to pick up your phone and dial 15 different lenders in your area. Fortunately for those of us without extra time on our hands, local Sunday papers quite often do this calling around for you. If you're Internet-equipped, you can review rates on your computer at any time, day or night. Or, order HSH Associates' Homebuyer's Mortgage Kit by calling 800-873-2837. The kit reports on about 80 lenders, depending on the area covered. You'll find information on interest rates, points, application fees, and other fees charged by each lender. This information is updated weekly.

In addition to the mortgage rate, pay attention to lists that mention application fees, points, and so on; they should all be right there in the same list. The bank with the best mortgage rate is not always the best place to go; it may charge higher fees in other areas.

When you're shopping around for a good mortgage, one of the most important parts of the loan is the interest rate. A 30-year fixed rate $125,000 mortgage at

QUICK 𝕟 PAINLESS

Check out the Mortgage Rate Shopper offered by the United Homeowners Association on the UHA Web site. Post your ideal mortgage here, and mortgage brokers will let you know if they have your kind of loan!

6 percent will have a monthly payment of $749. At 8 percent, it rises to $917; 10 percent costs $1,097 a month, and 12 percent will be $1,285 a month. You can see that over a number of years, the interest on higher rates is exorbitant.

Common sense tells you that the higher the interest rate on your mortgage, the more you pay in total cost for your home. Look at the differences:

Interest rate	Term	Monthly payment	Total
6.5%	15 years	$871.11	$ 56.799.80
6.5%	30 years	$632.07	$127,545.60
7.5%	15 years	$927.01	$66,861.80
7.5%	30 years	$699.21	$151,715.60
10.00%	15 years	$1,074.61	$93,429.80
10.00%	30 years	$877.57	$215,925.20

One of the smartest—and easiest—ways to save money when you're buying a house is to think about making bimonthly mortgage payments. Instead of paying 12 installment payments each year, you pay the bank 26 smaller payments (not 24). Biweekly payments are deducted automatically from your checking or savings account.

With this system, you repay a 30-year mortgage in a little less than 23 years, and a 15-year mortgage in 11 years. There's a significant savings in the total interest you'll be paying over the life of the loan. Not every bank offers biweekly payment plans; if your bank doesn't, you can get the same benefit if you make one extra principal payment a year on your mortgage.

Pre-qualification

If you really want to save time and energy, take advantage of your bank's pre-qualification plan. Pre-qualification is sort of like early admission to college; you fill out the forms and you know ahead of time that you're guaranteed of getting approved for a loan of a certain size.

This means you know exactly what you can and can't afford, so you won't waste time pressing your nose against the windows of mansions you can't buy. Pre-qualification also speeds up the mortgage approval period, since you have already given the bank your financial information. You also may come up with a stronger contract with better terms, since the sellers know you are a serious buyer who can afford their home.

To speed up the mortgage process, you should bring to the first appointment the following:

- last year's W-2s
- documents showing two years of residence and employment history (including canceled checks for mortgage or rent payments)
- proof of your gross monthly income (by bringing current pay stubs), with your employer's address and telephone number
- financial statements for your personal assets

QUICK ᴍ PAINLESS

If you add just $25 a month to a 30-year fixed rate 8-percent mortgage, you save $23,337 in interest over the life of the loan. If you can pay an extra $100 a month, you'll save $62,456!

Your monthly payments including principal, interest, insurance, and real estate taxes shouldn't be more than 28 percent of your household income. You shouldn't be paying more than 36 percent of your total income in mortgage and all other debts combined, including car payments and college loans.

- your last three tax returns
- list of assets including loans and deposit account numbers (bring along the last monthly statement available on each account)
- deed (if refinancing)
- for a construction loan, a fixed price contract, specifications, plans, and agreement of sale

Title Time

When it comes to title insurance, it pays to shop around. Ask your realtor as well as the mortgage company to provide you with the names of three title companies they know and like. Lenders and realtors know who is competent and efficient. Ask how title insurance is priced, and comparison shop for the ancillary fees the title company charges, such as a deed preparation fee or a tax certificate. You probably won't need an attorney if the title company prepares the deed and handles settlement.

If You've Been Turned Down . . .

If your bank says "thanks, but no thanks" to your mortgage application, find out why the loan was denied. If you don't qualify for the mortgage because your eyes were bigger than your purse, look for a less expensive home. If you have credit problems, talk with the lender and find out how you can qualify. Should you pay off some of your debt? Make set payments for a year or so to provide a credit history?

THE MONEY YOU SAVE COULD BE YOUR OWN . . .

One of the easiest ways to save money when it comes to real estate is to refinance your mortgage when interest rates drop 1.5 percent below the rate you're paying. Some mortgage officers say you should consider refinancing when rates drop as little as 1 percent, depending on whether interest rates are heading back up, how much you need the money, and how long you will be in your home to recoup the refinancing charges.

But mortgages aren't the only costly item you have to contend with. Real estate taxes are another big-ticket item too many people try to ignore. If you think you're paying too much for your taxes, you're not alone. You and the other 60 percent of Americans whose homes are over-assessed *can* do something about it, according to the National Taxpayers Union. Americans are a meek bunch overall, it seems. Most of us law-abiding citizens just accept our assessments at face value, assuming we can't fight city hall, and slink off to the bank to withdraw more money to pay our tax bills. Stop right there!

You can fight city hall, and what's even better, it's not that hard. Get a copy of your assessment at your local assessor's office (or the local library). Check it for accuracy. Are the lot size, square footage, and number of rooms correct? If there are any errors, or the local real estate values have fallen and the assessments haven't, you can challenge the assessment. You don't even have to hire a lawyer.

QUICK ◖■◗ *PAINLESS*

Keep an eye on those mortgage interest rates! Refinancing when they drop will save you a lot down the road!

INVESTING IN REAL ESTATE

If you've got time and money to burn, buying a getaway place in the country for weekends and holidays may look like a good idea. But if you're like the rest of us and barely have time to brush your teeth before flying off to work, you may want to rethink this particular dream.

Vacation homes can be a good investment, but they take up an awful lot of time. If you're thinking about a vacation home, you owe it to yourself to consider the outlay—mortgage payments, real estate taxes, upkeep, insurance, expenditures (new roof, painting, and so on)—before deciding you can afford a second home. The good news: You can deduct the interest on a mortgage on a second home, so this lowers your current income tax liability.

If you decide you can afford it, next ask yourself if you *want* to afford it. Your vacation home will determine your vacation for many years; and just like your primary residence, vacation real estate always seems to require money for a new project or unexpected expense. And who's going to mow the lawn, do the landscaping, paint the walls, and fuss with the tricky toilet that never wants to flush?

If you still want a vacation home but you don't want the hassle of upkeep, you could think about a condo or do what lots of other folks with no spare time do—choose a time share. Time shares have gotten a bad rep from folks who've been roped into listening to one of those nauseating sales pitches, but they actually are very interesting and imaginative products. However, they're not really an investment—they are more of a rental agreement with a company for vacation property. There are still annual fees and transfer expenses, but you do save considerable time since you're not responsible for maintaining the property. For this reason, they could be a good choice for folks without lots of extra time to fuss.

If you can get the time share for a reasonable price, and you use it frequently to travel to many different areas, it can save you money on your trips. Comparison shop and review the situation with a time-share realtor in the area you are looking into—not through the time-share company itself.

While we're talking about investments, there are some folks who wonder whether buying and selling real estate might be the path to riches. Keep in mind, however, that just because an investment is in real estate doesn't mean it can't be a poor investment. Real estate prices tend to move up or down depending on the economy and which geographic areas are growing. The interest rate environment, your local job market, and the general economy at the present time are all considerations, because to make money, rental property needs renters. You need income coming in to help pay the expenses of the property.

To determine if real estate is a good investment, take the rental income, deduct your expenses, and see what the rate of return is before and after taxes. Remember that your funds are at risk and the investment is long term, and not liquid. Rents may be stable, but taxes, utilities, and other related expenses are often rising, so the

YOU'LL THANK YOURSELF LATER

Before you buy a time share, check around to see if you can buy a used one from a previous owner. You can often save thousands of dollars this way. You'll find extensive lists of time shares for sale and rent on the Internet.

total return on real estate may not be as lucrative as it once was.

Most important, as a person without a lot of extra time, do you really want to spend all those weekends fixing up the rental property, dealing with complaints, and hassling people to send their rent checks in on time?

Congratulations! You've successfully navigated the real estate market! So enjoy your new neighborhood and have some lemonade on your new front porch!

Getting Time on Your Side

	The Old Way	The Lazy Way
Getting your house ready to sell on the outside	1 month	1 weekend
Getting your house ready to sell on the inside	1 month	1 weekend
Comparing mortgage rates	2 hours	3 minutes
Choosing an agent	3 weeks	1 week
Paying of your mortgage	Up to 30 years	Half the time
Finding the right home for you	2 months	1 month

Chapter
fourteen

Relaxing Retirement Planning

We're all busy. We work hard all day, then try to juggle housework and child care and tend to a thousand-and-one other responsibilities. Who has time or energy left over to think about putting together a retirement plan?

In fact, that's exactly what more than half of all Americans say; fewer than 50 percent of us have put aside any money specifically for retirement. As of 1993, one-third of workers who had access to a 401(k) plan didn't participate.

You say you don't like to think too much about investments? You don't have the time to fuss with money management? No problem. You can still save money for your retirement. You'd be surprised at the number of ways there are for you to automatically save money for retirement without having to lift a finger. And the sooner you start, the more money you'll have.

If you stick $2,000 into an IRA at age 18 and never add any more, averaging 10 percent a year you will have $176,400 at age 65. Bingo! No muss, no fuss, and a nice sum of money at the end. If you invest $2,000 each year from age 18 to age 65, you will have $1,744,000 at age 65. Now there's an advertisement for compounding! All without your having to worry about selling or trading anything.

Although these numbers seem unreal (and they are not adjusted for inflation), they are accurate. It is never too soon to start saving for retirement. You should begin no later than age 35.

This doesn't mean that if you're teetering on the far side of 43 you should just give up. Saving something is always better than saving nothing, no matter when you begin. Ideally, you'll need about 70 percent of your pre-retirement income in order to maintain your standard of living once you stop working. When figuring out how much you'll need, first you need to figure out how much of the money you've been paying to the government is going to be given back to you.

Social Security provides up to 45 percent of the wage replacement ratio for a single lower-income worker who retires at the age of 65. If this worker is married to someone who never worked outside the home, the wage replacement ratio increases to 76 percent of the pre-retirement income. If you've earned a high income, this ratio is quite different. In this case, Social Security will replace only 13.5 percent of your pre-retirement income. The ratio increases to 20.25 if you have a nonworking spouse.

Still, it helps to know exactly what's coming. (And those of you who emphatically believe Social Security

IF YOU'RE SO
INCLINED

Invest in an IRA and sit back while it works for you. Look Ma! No stocks to track!

will self-destruct before you reach retirement age should definitely be saving.) The government keeps records of how much money you've invested in Social Security from every job you've ever held. All of us should check our Social Security accounts every three years to make sure that everything is accurate. If the information in your records is incorrect, you need to know about it so it can be corrected and your benefits will be accurate.

Social Security was never designed to be a retiree's full wage replacement, and as you can see, it probably won't meet all your retirement needs. That's why it's important to plan how you will supplement your benefits. There are a few more things you can do now that don't take up much time, but that can help you prepare for an easier retirement:

- Learn about your employer's pension or profit-sharing plan. For a free booklet on private pensions, call the U.S. Department of Labor at 800-998-7542 or ask for publication 590 from the IRS by calling 800-829-3676.

- Contribute to a tax-sheltered savings plan, such as a 401(k). Ask your employer to start a plan if there isn't one in place.

- Put money into an IRA.

- If you change jobs, roll your IRA over into your new employer's retirement plan.

- Set goals and stick to them. The sooner you start saving, the more time you have to gain interest.

QUICK ⬤ PAINLESS

You can get a copy of your estimated benefits by calling the Social Security hotline at 800-772-1213. You'll be guided by a taped message into leaving your name and address, and within two weeks you'll receive a form to request your records. For even quicker results, visit their Web site at http://www. ssa.gov.

People whose adjusted gross income exceeds the earnings ceiling may contribute after-tax income to a nonde-ductible IRA, even if they *are* covered by a retirement plan at work. They pay taxes on earnings only after reaching age 59½.

Ask questions. Get information from your employer, bank, union, or financial advisor.

Your financial advisor should have the software to help guide you into figuring out how much you need to contribute to a retirement plan to guarantee you're comfortable at retirement. The Vanguard investment firm has software available at a very reasonable cost so that you can do the projections yourself (800-523-7077), but remember the projections are based on assumptions.

INDIVIDUAL RETIREMENT ACCOUNTS (IRAS)

If it's investment ease you're looking for, look no farther than an IRA. An IRA is a personal pension account to set aside money for retirement; you can contribute up to $2,000 in pretax income to a deductible IRA each year if your employer doesn't offer a pension or a tax-deferred retirement/savings plan and if you meet certain income limits. You pay federal and state income tax on the investment interest only when you withdraw the money after you reach age 59½. There are numerous rules and regulations set up by the government, but all growth and income on an IRA is tax deferred.

More affluent wage earners who didn't qualify to deduct contributions to an IRA will now be able to get their tax break with a Roth IRA. These new IRAs are available to:

- singles with an adjusted gross income less than $95,000

- couples filing "married filing jointly" earning less than $150,000

The major difference between a traditional IRA and the new Roth IRAs is that there is no tax of any kind on withdrawals as long as some money has been in the account for at least five years and the account holder is $59\frac{1}{2}$. Unless you die, become disabled, or are making a first-home purchase, early withdrawal will be subject to state and federal income taxes and a 10-percent penalty.

While you must take distributions from a traditional IRA account by age $70\frac{1}{2}$, there is no mandatory distribution date for a Roth IRA. You can leave your money in place as long as you live.

An IRA is a good idea even if you already have investments in a 401(k) at work. First you should make sure you maximize your 401(k) "matchable" contributions. After that, if you can afford the extra $2,000 a year, get a Roth IRA. If $2,000 is too much, contribute what funds you can afford. Remember that by setting funds aside, you are contributing to your financial security at retirement.

Higher-income investors who aren't eligible to have tax-deductible IRAs because they earn too much money should open Roth IRAs. Generally, Roth IRAs seem preferable if you must wait a long time until retirement, since your buildup in earnings will be tax free. The Roth IRA is better if you believe your income tax bracket will stay the same or even increase after retirement.

Anyone whose adjusted gross income is less than $100,000 can transfer funds from a current tax-deferred

A COMPLETE WASTE OF TIME

The 3 Worst Things to Do When Investing:

1. Choose an investment plan that requires more time than you have.

2. Invest without researching what you're really getting into.

3. Don't invest for your future at all.

The 10-percent penalty for early IRA withdrawals is waived for funds used for education from all IRAs (even current IRAs), but you still have to pay income tax on withdrawals for education. The amount of the withdrawal is unlimited.

IRA to a Roth IRA, making all future growth of that retirement account permanently tax free. This makes sense if you are young and have decades to allow your Roth IRA funds to accumulate. The difference can add up to thousands of dollars of extra income in retirement. You can transfer the funds by paying income tax on what is in the current IRA (payment on this can be made over a four-year period) and transferring the funds. You need to carefully consider this move, and you should have your financial advisor analyze whether this is the best move for you.

IF YOU'RE SELF-EMPLOYED . . .

If you're self-employed, you may be interested in a SEP-IRA. Many banks, mutual fund companies, and insurance companies offer SEP services and should be able to help you sort through your options. Call your local IRS office for a copy of form 5305-SEP or 5305-SIMPLE.

Self-employed people also may set up a Keogh plan. They require more paperwork to set up than does a SEP, but they let you put away a higher percent of your income (20 percent) up to a maximum of $30,000 per year.

401(K) PLANS

Another effortless way of saving money is to have payments automatically deducted from your paycheck at work, as part of a 401(k) plan. Your contributions are made before being taxed and are sometimes matched by employers. 401(k)s have become very popular in recent years because of employees' ability to transfer their funds from employer to employer or employer to IRA. Employees also like the choices of internal funds usually allowed by the plan.

The maximum contribution made to a 401(k) plan was $9,500 in 1997, but this maximum can be lowered if there are more higher-salaried employees contributing to the plan than lower-salaried employees. It's imperative that you contribute enough to get all company-matched funds. Beyond that amount, you should contribute as much as you can afford per pay period, gradually increasing the contribution with raises. It's amazing how little you will miss money from your paycheck if you don't see it.

You can't afford not to contribute if you want security in your retirement. A $1,000 contribution for someone in the 28 percent bracket is really only a $720 contribution (because you're saving $280 in tax by making the deductible contribution).

Start with a small contribution and gradually increase it; you can start at $50 a month and work up to $2,000 a year. Or start at a contribution of 3 percent of your income, and work up to the maximum amount for your plan.

MUTUAL FUNDS

Another nice investment for money managers without a lot of time on their hands is a mutual fund, a company that pools the money of many investors and invests it in stocks, bonds, or other securities. The good news is that

YOU'LL THANK YOURSELF LATER

Protecting your future shouldn't damage your present. Invest what you can afford now— you can always invest more later.

with a mutual fund, you don't have to spend time doing all the research for individual stocks or securities. Mutual funds are managed by portfolio managers and a research team whose job it is to screen investments for those that best meet the objectives of the fund. The portfolio team visits companies, analyzes reports, and spends all its time in research. Fund managers are usually graduates of top business schools.

Because each fund is managed by a professional, who does the research and selects the investments, there is far less time needed than if you were investing in the individual stocks, bonds, or securities yourself.

Each fund has its own objectives, but a specific rate of return isn't guaranteed. Most financial advisors do suggest that you invest in more than one fund, so that if one of your funds is down it won't affect all your money.

We know, we know. You don't have time to sift through all those funds? No problem! Several companies offer software to help you pick a mutual fund. Programs will search for funds in certain sectors, such as health, no-load (no commission) funds, and so on.

- Ascent (Morningstar) leads you through mutual fund selection with text and onscreen help. Call 800-735-0700 for more information.

- Mutual Fund Expert covers more than 10,000 funds; it costs $50 for the basic version, $107 for a quarterly updated version, and $220 for the deluxe monthly updates. Call 800-379-0679 for more information.

- No-Load Analyzer for Windows contains all of the above information, together with 50 stocks held in each fund portfolio. Call 800-284-7607 for more information.

Alternatively, you can visit a host of sites on the Web to find more information on mutual funds. These include:

- Strong Funds (http://www.strongfunds.com) is an investment company who's Web site provides basic information on their family of funds.

- IBC Financial Data (http://www.ibcdata.com) lists money market funds and provides general guidance on investment and retirement, with data on the funds' past performance.

- T. Rowe Price (http://www.troweprice.com) is another mutual fund Web site that specializes in no-loads. The site provides performance data on a variety of possible investment funds.

- Microsoft Investor (http://www.investor.msn.com) lists data on mutual fund companies that offer retirement planning details.

- Mutual Funds Interactive (http://www.fundsinteractive.com) offers news and information about mutual funds.

- Nest Egg (http://www.nestegg.com) provides news on mutual funds and can help calculate the best amount to save for retirement.

- Net Results (http://isnetwork.com) helps you put together a diversified portfolio of no-load mutual

IF YOU'RE SO
INCLINED

Jump into the Web to learn about your options; you can only come away with a better idea of what your money can do for you!

funds for a yearly subscription of $149.

- PR Newswire (http://www.pmewswire.com) offers an online money magazine and financial press releases, as well as links to a variety of financial sites.

Another nice thing about mutual funds is that you don't need a lot of money to invest. Many of the no-load funds waive the $1,000 minimum if you agree to invest $50 a month (that's just $11.54 a week) automatically from your bank account.

Firms that offer automatic investment programs for minimums of $50 include:

- Invesco funds, in Denver (800-525-8085)
- T. Rowe Price funds, in Baltimore (800-638-5660)
- American Century funds, in Kansas City (800-345-2021)
- Strong funds, in Milwaukee (800-638-1030)

There are a variety of types of investments. Here are a few, beginning with the most conservative:

- **Blue chip funds.** If you invest in mutual funds that buy blue chip companies when they are temporarily depressed, you can make money. Try the no-load Neuberger & Berman Focus (800-877-9700) at a $50 monthly minimum.

- **Mid-cap stocks.** These midsize companies have passed through the risky initial start-up phase, but haven't quite made it to "blue chip" status. These so-called "mid-cap" stocks are usually less risky than smaller companies, but they have more potential

YOU'LL THANK YOURSELF LATER

Before you make your decision, you should read all parts of the mutual fund prospectus, which will discuss the risks, investment goals, and policies of the fund.

than blue chips. Over the past 10 years, they've gained about 15.7 percent each year. For a good mutual fund that invests primarily in this category, try T. Rowe Price Mid-Cap Growth (800-638-5660) at a $50 monthly minimum.

- **Small company stocks.** Firms with less than $500 million in annual sales can consistently deliver a solid 12-percent return, which makes them good for a long-term savings plan. Try Founders Discovery (800-525-2440) at a $50 monthly minimum.

- **Emerging market funds.** Today's emerging markets in Latin America and Asia can offer a good profit potential, but there is much more risk than for a blue chip stock. There may be incredible swings in price, but there are opportunities as well. Try T. Rowe Price Emerging Markets Stock Fund (800-638-5660) for a $50 monthly minimum.

- **Gold funds.** Mutual funds that invest in gold-mining shares could deliver big profits; funds that invest in gold mining around the world are safer than those that concentrate on one country alone. Try Scudder Gold (800-225-2470), with a $1,000 minimum.

- **Technology funds.** If you're a computer nerd or you think technology can maintain its strong performance, you might enjoy the mutual funds that focus on new technology. There are risks, but there is also good opportunity. Try Invesco Strategic Technology (800-525-8085) at a $50 monthly minimum.

QUICK **n** PAINLESS

If you invest $50 a month in a no-load mutual fund and your investments earn a conservative 12% a year, you'll have more than $10,000 in 10 years.

BONDS

Bonds are the most common lending investment traded on a securities market. When a bond is issued, it has a specific maturity date at which you will be repaid your principal. Bonds fluctuate in value, primarily based on interest rate changes. (If you have a bond worth 7 percent and the interest rates rise to 11 percent, your bond decreases in value—no one would want to buy your bond when they could get one at a higher interest rate.)

There are many different kinds of bonds:

- U.S. Treasury notes and bonds
- U.S. savings bonds
- U.S. government agency issues
- municipal bonds
- corporate bonds
- mortgage-backed securities and CMOs
- convertible bonds
- certificates of deposit
- bond mutual funds

The safest investment is a three-month Treasury bill, an obligation of the U.S. Treasury; it's considered risk free. This statement is based on the security of the underlying investment, not taking into consideration inflation or real return after taxes.

Stocks

Stock is the most common ownership investment traded on the securities market. When you buy stock, you are

IF YOU'RE SO
INCLINED

If you want to check your mutual funds quickly, try online Web sites at Morningstar, Valueline, Micropal, and CDA/Weisenberger. They all monitor mutual fund prices and performance.

buying an interest in a specific business. Stocks represent ownership shares in a corporation and may pay dividends, whereas bonds pay interest over a specific period of time.

Over the past 65 years, common stocks have returned an average of 12 percent each year. For this reason, advisors believe that there's a good chance that a well-diversified portfolio, which includes average-risk common stocks, will continue to bring in about 12 percent a year. You make money on your investment if the company pays a dividend or if the company's stock increases in value.

While stocks can get really complicated, lazy money managers will be happy to hear that Internet trading is now available. Considerably cheaper than traditional trading, it's also a lot faster, and it's much easier to make comparisons between brokers.

When you trade online, you get a status report when you make the online order, and you'll receive a monthly statement. These days, if you're inclined to do your own research, most of the information you need is available online. When you've done your research and are ready to buy stock, you need either a traditional or discount broker. Stock prices can range from less than $1 to more than $100 per share.

Like anything in life, you usually get what you pay for. If you use a full-service house, you'll get personalized attention and personalized research, investment ideas or information, and financial planning services. A discount broker just makes the trades you request.

A COMPLETE WASTE OF TIME

The 3 Worst Things to Do with Your Stocks:

1. Ignore them.

2. Buy high risk when you don't know what you're getting into.

3. Ignore the assets to Internet trading.

There's quite a difference in price: On a comparable trade, prices might range from a low of $14.95 to $150. You can shop from one discount broker to another, but it's very hard to make good cost comparisons, since they all use secret algorithms that factor in a variety of variables. Others online discount brokers such as E*Trade charge a flat rate (usually about $20) per transaction.

There are many popular online brokers available. Here's a list of some of the most popular:

- AccuTrade (http://www.accutrade.com) provides a wide range of investment options, including stocks, bonds, options, mutual funds, and foreign securities. A new account requires an initial deposit of $5,000.

- American Express Financial Direct (http://www.americanexpress.com/direct) is associated with other American Express services and offers information about annuities, money market funds, and mutual funds. Their InvestDirect is a trading account with no access to research; there is no minimum deposit and commissions are $26.95 per trade. The InvestDirect/Power Tools includes news and research; commissions are higher and there is a $5,000 minimum.

- Aufhauser (http://www.aufhauser.com) lets you make up to 20 trades a month for a flat fee of $800 a year. The company offers equities, options, and funds.

- Ceres Securities (http://www.ceres.com) is a discount broker offering online stock trading and some research, together with a calculator that lets you compare Ceres' rates with those of other brokers. There's a flat $18 commission per trade.

- DATEK Online (http://www.datek.com) is a discount broker that charges just $9.99 for online trades ($2,000 minimum), but trading is limited to only certain stock exchanges. Higher rates apply for telephone trades.

- eBroker (http://www.ebroker.com) offers equity trades at $12 a share, with a minimum $10,000 deposit required to open a new account. This discount broker offers no research and no tools.

- e.Schwab (http://www.eschwab.com) offers quotes, news and research, and stock trading at $29.95 for stock trades up to 1,000 shares, and 3 cents a share for anything over that. There's a minimum deposit of $5,000 for investment, custodial, or trust accounts and $2,000 for IRAs.

- Fidelity Investments (http://personal.fidelity.com/brokerage) offers special discounts ($25 a transaction) to active traders (trading more than 36 times a year), with online trading of stocks and bonds.

- PC Financial Network (http://www.pcfn.com), traders in stocks, options, mutual funds, and Treasury products, offer stock quotes, alerts, and reports for members. The standard commission is $39.95 per trade; frequent traders get a small discount.

YOU'LL THANK YOURSELF LATER

Be sure to check out any online brokerage thoroughly before doing business with them. A pretty Web page doesn't necessarily mean the brokerage is honest.

■ Wall Street Access Online (http://www.wsaccess.com) allows you to place equity and options orders and access account information through its Web site.

Once you open an account with an online stockbroker, you can pay for the transactions in several ways:

■ wire funds

■ direct deposit

■ online cash transfer (you can set up an electronic transfer from any check-writing account to your brokerage)

Congratulations! You've invested wisely! Now sit back and enjoy a latte . . . you deserve it!

The Lazy Way

Getting Time on Your Side

	The Old Way	The Lazy Way
Trading stock	15 minutes	2 minutes
Researching investments	1 day	30 minutes
Comparing brokers	3 hours	5 minutes
Tracking stocks	2 hours	2 minutes
Preparing for your future	1 year	A weekend
Purchasing stocks	30 minutes	10 minutes

If There's a Will, I Want to Be in It

Let's face it: We all have to go sometime, and when we do, we can't drag our stuff along with us. The act of writing a will itself isn't hard, and if push comes to shove, a few lines scribbled on a piece of paper will save your heirs a whole lot of hassle.

For some reason, 70 percent of Americans have concluded that the lazy way to handle the problem of a will is not to write one at all. That may save a few hours and momentary headaches now, but it's guaranteed to subject your heirs to days, weeks, and months of unbelievable aggravation.

The key to handling an estate the lazy way is to arrange things so that your heirs won't have to spend the rest of their lives getting your property through probate. It's a sort of second-hand, long-distance lazy way of arranging your affairs, making it easier on your friends and family left behind.

The best, the easiest, and the most important way to ensure that your estate will be settled smoothly is to prepare a will in the first place.

Now.

Right this minute.

Drop what you're doing, sit down, and start writing.

For many people, the act of writing a will seems a little creepy, sort of the way Ebenezer Scrooge felt when he peeped at his own gravestone from beneath the skirts of the Ghost of Christmas Future. It's hard to accept that we're going to die, and writing a will just makes it all too real for some folks. Those whose lives are already filled to the brim can convince themselves they don't have time to make the effort.

But as usual, spending a few moments today can save enormous hours farther down the road for somebody else you care about.

FIRST THINGS FIRST

This may seem obvious, but before you begin making plans, you need to know what assets and liabilities you have (in other words, what's coming in and what's going out). Spend a few minutes writing down your assets and your debts. The process of estate planning begins by knowing where you are now.

There are three documents you should keep in your estate planning file to make it easier on your heirs:

- Power of Attorney
- Living will
- Will

If you have dependent children, a will is crucial if you want to name a guardian for them. Do you really want the courts to decide who will take care of your children if you and your spouse die before they reach adulthood?

If you're a single parent and you die without a will, your children may have to get a court order to open your safety deposit boxes. If you die without a will, the state will appoint an administrator to supervise the distribution of your assets—costing about 5 percent of the value of your estate. The administrator also must post a bond, which costs another several hundred dollars. If you die without a will, the state steps in and divides your property for you according to state law. In this case, odds are your favorite third cousin, a beloved charity, or close friends will likely get nothing.

COMPUTER WILLS GIVE YOU MORE TIME!

When it comes to writing a will, of course the very easiest, least time-consuming way is to hire a lawyer. However, with today's computer software packages, it's not much more difficult and time-consuming to write your own.

Odds are, the attorney you pay to write your will won't sit at a desk and write the thing out longhand: Most likely, she will simply enter your information in the company computer, using the latest will-writing software. Most attorneys prepare wills using these software packages.

A will is made valid not because it is prepared by an attorney, but because it is witnessed by three people who can attest that you weren't crazy when you wrote it

QUICK **n** PAINLESS

If you can't make up your mind right now who should raise your kids if you die, appoint a trust guardian today who could decide for you if you die before you get around to writing a will.

If you have more than $600,000 in your estate (the level at which federal estate taxes kick in), writing your own will may not be a good idea. In this case, use an attorney to prepare your will.

and nobody was holding a gun to your head to make you sign.

So far, computer-generated wills have not caused any legal problems in those cases where they have been used, and if you're not going to hire an attorney, they are probably the easiest way to go.

Those of you with limited time and limited funds will be happy to hear there's another choice besides hiring an attorney (expensive) or doing it yourself (more time-consuming): You can hire a paralegal to help you prepare the documents. The National Association for Independent Paralegals (707-935-7951) can refer you to paralegals in your area. Check it out!

WRITTEN AND THEN FORGOTTEN?

Writing a will is sort of like getting a root canal: Once it's done, most people try to put it out of their minds and forget about it. However, if you're intent on getting through life with the least amount of hassle, the last thing you want to do with a will is forget it exists.

This is especially true if you wrote a will and then got married. Most people don't realize that the moment you say "I do," any will you had before the nuptials automatically becomes invalid. If you have the misfortune to die soon after you get married and before you've had a chance to make a new will, the court will treat your estate as if you had never made a will at all. As a result, any of your special bequests might not be carried out.

The danger here is not that your new spouse won't inherit your property—in most cases, he or she will—but that any special requests you had included in your old will might not be honored. You may have had some very good reasons for wanting to reward that sweet little man on the pastry cart who always saved the best glazed donut for you, but odds are the court isn't going to know or care. Many people figure their old will is good enough to "tide them over" until they get around to having a new will made. It's just not true.

Many folks have lots of individual pieces of property—Great Aunt Sarah's gold brooch, Uncle Bill's complete collection of *National Geographics*, and so on—that would take a great deal of time and energy to insert into a will. Plus, any change in how this property should be divided means an entire new will would have to be made.

The easiest way to handle this is to make a list of your personal property and attach it to your will, with a clause in your will distributing the property according to the list. This way, if your niece runs off with that grunge musician wearing a ring in his nose, you can transfer her share of the family jewels to someone else without having to write a new will. It makes things a lot easier if you change your mind about who should get what.

Technically, if you hold everything jointly with your spouse, you could get away without having a will, especially if your estate totals less than $625,000. But you never know what the future holds, and it's imperative to have a will if you have minor children in case you both die in a common accident.

YOU'LL THANK YOURSELF LATER

You should review your will:

- whenever family circumstances change
- when there are major changes in tax law
- if you have a major change in your business

EXECUTOR: CHOOSING THE ONE IN CHARGE

When you are making your will, you'll have to choose an executor—the person responsible for settling your estate. The field is fairly broad: You may choose anyone who hasn't been convicted of a felony. Most folks select their spouse, adult child, another relative, or a friend.

Some people name their accountant or attorney as executor. But what if you die on April 3? That's busy tax season for an accountant. What if your attorney is caught up in an important case? You want to choose someone who has the time to work for you.

It's a good idea to ask the person you want to have as executor if he or she will accept. Being an executor is a lot of work. The person will have to track down lots of details, and may even need to help defend the terms of the will against squabbling heirs. And by the way, it's not a good idea to sign up all of your children as co-executors; settling an estate by committee can be a nightmare. The executor doesn't need to be a son or the eldest child, either—just a person who is responsible, who will follow your instructions, who lives nearby (if possible), and who will administer the estate "according to law." The person doesn't even need to be family—just someone you trust.

IF YOU'VE INHERITED THE JOB . . .

Executor is not a cushy job, and it's not for the lazy or faint of heart. It can be time-consuming, especially if the estate is large or there are any problems. The executor is legally obligated to act in the interests of the deceased, and to follow that person's wishes contained in the will.

An executor's duties include:

- finding the will
- hiring a lawyer (if necessary)
- applying to appear before probate court
- notifying beneficiaries named in the will
- arranging for publication of "notice to creditors" and mailing a copy to each creditor
- sending notice of the person's death to the post office, utilities, banks, credit card companies, and so on
- inventorying assets and having them appraised
- collecting debts owed to the estate
- identifying any unpaid salary, insurance, and employee benefits
- filing for life insurance and benefits
- filing for city, state, and federal tax and estate tax returns
- paying claims against the estate
- distributing assets and getting receipts from beneficiaries
- filing papers to finalize the estate

It sounds like a lot of work, and it is. Because of this, executors can receive a percentage of the estate for their trouble, although most states have set limits on the amount. Because the payment is compensation, it's

YOU'LL THANK YOURSELF LATER

The duties of an executor are legion, but the lazy way to handle them is to hire an attorney to help. The attorney's fees can be charged to the estate as expenses of administration. For your own protection, you should keep copies of all records for at least two years.

subject to income tax, although it isn't subject to self-employment tax (unless you are in the estate settlement business). If you are an heir and an executor, it's not a good idea to take the fee unless the amount of money you'd pay in death taxes is higher than your personal income tax bracket.

If you are the executor but not an heir and you've done the work and assumed the responsibility, you should take the fee. Moreover, an executor is usually entitled to be reimbursed from the estate for expenses incurred in settling. For example, if you live in Maine and you must settle an estate in California, the estate would pay for your commute.

LIVING WELL WITH A LIVING WILL

Once your will is written, it's time to think about putting together a living will. Also known in legal circles as an advance directive, a living will outlines how you want to be treated if you become profoundly ill or irreversibly incompetent and need life support systems or heroic measures to keep you alive. It spells out to your doctor, the hospital, your family, and anybody else concerned what measures may and may not be taken so that you may be allowed to die with dignity and without unwanted intervention. Since you may not have time to go through the hassle of dealing with an attorney for a living will, we've included samples of a living will/health directive in Chapter 1.

QUICK **IT** PAINLESS

To make things easy:

- Place all your important documents in a safety deposit box.

- Keep a list of the contents at home.

- Tell family or your executor where your lock-box key is.

POWER UP WITH A POA

While you're putting together your will and living will, you'll want to think about setting up a Power of Attorney (POA), a legally recognized transfer of authority to another person. This is the third thing you can do to streamline your life the lazy way, because if you become unable to handle your affairs and you don't have a POA, life will become a monumental hassle.

It's important to grant a Power of Attorney so that someone you choose can handle your affairs if you become incompetent or incapacitated. Otherwise, the court would appoint a guardian, and who wants dreadful Aunt Elizabeth to step in and mess with your life? Most people don't realize that if you're married and you become incapacitated, your spouse won't be able to make those decisions for you without a Power of Attorney.

The powers that you grant to someone else can be broad or very specific:

- A personal POA gives your agent the right to make decisions about medical care.

- A financial POA gives your agent the power to handle your financial decisions. If you had a stroke, your spouse couldn't access your personal checking account to pay your bills without a financial POA.

- A medical POA grants authority to someone you trust to make decisions with a physician about your medical care options.

IF YOU'RE SO
INCLINED

Lots of people, thinking they've arranged things the lazy way, say they don't need a will because they've given a child Power of Attorney. Wrong! A Power of Attorney ends at the moment of death. When the POA ceases, the assets become part of a probate estate.

Have your child be a deputy, not an owner, of your safety deposit box. A surviving spouse can enter a jointly owned box, but if there is a third party's name on it, the death of any of the owners seals the box.

A standard POA gives your agent the right to make decisions in all areas of your life. You and your spouse each need a standard POA for the other. (No time to consult a lawyer for a POA?

PAY BEFORE YOU GO: WILL IT REALLY SAVE YOU TIME?

Some folks, thinking they'll make things easier on their heirs, prepay their funeral expenses. But unless the funds are delegated to a burial reserve fund independent of any corporation, it's not a good idea to pay for your funeral ahead of time. However, it *is* a good idea to make funeral plans with the funeral director of your choice and let your family know what you want. This guarantees you get the funeral that you desire—not one planned with guilt or emotion. You'll probably be more financially sensible with your funeral than your children would be. If there is to be a service, let your children know who you would like for pallbearers and what hymns and scripture you want.

If you want to save all the time and energy of funerals, viewings, and burial, you can be cremated through the American Crematory Society. However, funeral directors can still be very helpful with the details, such as the number of death certificates you will need, newspaper announcements, and so on. Ask your funeral director what his fees are, and then comparison shop.

LIVING TRUSTS

While you're thinking about putting your affairs in order, spend some time thinking about setting up a living trust. A living trust transfers assets into a trust: You control the assets, and you can revoke the trust if you wish. The advantage of a living trust is that when you die, the assets pass directly to your beneficiaries without going through probate. This is inheritance the lazy way, since it avoids probate, which can be a long, costly hassle for your beneficiaries (and the lawyers may get between 5 and 7 percent of the value of the assets). Moreover, your assets become a matter of public record when the will is probated; the trust assets do not.

Of course, while living trusts keep assets out of probate, they don't lessen your tax burden. The person who benefits the most from a living trust is someone who is over age 60, not married, with assets above $100,000.

You don't need an attorney to prepare a living trust; you can use software or hire a paralegal. However, if you have a large estate (more than $600,000) and you don't have the time or expertise to worry about estate planning, a lawyer could be a good investment. They're not cheap, however. Attorney fees to set up a living trust may cost up to $2,000.

WENDING YOUR WAY THROUGH PROBATE

If you're an heir involved in tidying up an estate, no matter how lazy you may feel about the prospect, no matter how ardently you'd like to go to sleep and forget about

Congratulations! You've just signed your name at the bottom of your will. Now take a break! Go have that double chocolate fudge sundae with whipped cream and nuts. You can live dangerously now that you're protected.

it, eventually all of the estate's assets must be shuffled through a court process known as "probate"—the legal means for implementing the directions given in a will, and the formal process of proving its authenticity.

The easiest way to get through the process is to hire an attorney to do it for you. Trust us: It's the lazy way, and it's the best way.

You don't have to have an attorney for probate, but if you don't hire one you must be very careful to file all the right papers at the right time. The courthouse staff can guide you partway through the process, as can your accountant. But if you hit a problem, or if there is any real estate involved or you want someone to review your work, find an attorney who will charge you on an hourly basis. Good legal counsel is worth the money.

QUICK ‹ɪɪ› PAINLESS

Hiring an attorney to navigate your will through probate later will save everyone a lot of time and hassle.

Getting Time on Your Side

	The Old Way	The Lazy Way
Writing a will	2 hours	10 minutes
Writing a living will	1 hour	10 minutes
Writing a POA	1 hour	10 minutes
Keeping your will updated	An afternoon	10 minutes
Choosing an executor	Weeks	An afternoon
Planning the funeral	A week	An afternoon

sixteen

Cashing in on Computers

Y ou don't have time to research mutual funds? You can't keep track of expenses? You forgot to record the last couple of checks you wrote and you're afraid your checks are rubber? Sit down, put your feet up, and prepare to turn the job over to your computer.

The computer age is a dream come true for money managers without the inclination, energy, or time to track their own financial matters. At this moment, for example, there are nearly 2 million Americans who've opened online brokerage accounts. They're managing their money right now the easy way, and you can, too. With a computer, you can:

- Pay your bills
- Balance your checkbook
- Call up credit card records
- Find out your credit rating
- Get the best deal on a new car

- List a photo of your house for sale

- Get the best air fares

- Arrange to swap your vacation time share

- Look for a job

- Review your holdings 24 hours a day

- Advertise for a job

- Check out college costs

- Plan your retirement

- Buy stocks, bonds, and mutual funds

- Check out the reputation of your broker

And that's just the beginning! If it has to do with money, odds are there's a way to do it faster, cheaper, and better on a computer. So sit down, plug in your computer, and see how.

ELECTRONIC MAIL

You've already gotten lots of tips throughout this book about how to save money around the house. But here's something else to think about: Have you ever added up the money—and time—you spend buying stamps, envelopes, and paper? If you go through a book of stamps a week on personal mail, notes, letters, and cards, that's more than $25 a month. If you mail things overnight with a delivery service, that can add $10 or more per letter. And with the U.S. Postal System raising the postage rate every few moments, things are only going to get worse.

The solution to saving money and time? Electronic mail.

Whether you're a veteran computer hacker or an online novice, odds are you're already addicted to getting e-mail, because it's faster, cheaper, and just plain more fun than Snail Mail any day. In fact, it's safe to say that e-mail alone has revolutionized the world of personal and business communications. For the price of a monthly carrier fee, you can zip off an e-mail message to folks halfway across the world—without paying expensive long-distance rates or postage. Longer documents can be attached in disk form and zapped almost instantaneously into another person's computer, bypassing the need for expensive courier or delivery services.

This saves both money and time. You don't need to waste precious moments searching for envelopes, pen, and paper. You don't have to waste more tedious minutes looking up unfamiliar ZIP codes or addresses, or worry about whether the information will arrive in time and unscathed. You don't need to waste yet more time as you hop in the car and drive to the post office to buy stamps because your daughter used up the last ones mailing out that chain letter.

It's fast—hey, it's just about instantaneous. Several companies provide free "reminder" services, notifying you ahead of time via e-mail of important upcoming birthdays and other dates that you've set up. Other Web sites allow you to send "virtual greeting cards" (again, many are free!) via e-mail, for those folks who are too busy to go out and buy a card in time. Again, you're saving time and money by using the service.

A close relative to e-mail is the "instant message." If

A COMPLETE WASTE OF TIME

The 3 Worst Things to Do When Handling Your Money:

1. Don't use your computer.

2. Buy software that isn't right for you.

3. Assume the old way is the right way.

you feel like talking to your cousin in Ireland or your sister in Detroit, many online services allow you to send "instant messages" if both of you are online at the same time. You can simply type messages to each other via computer back and forth—for hours on end if you wish, all for the cost of a local call. And indications are that soon you'll be able to buy "virtual stamps" online and print them out on plain envelopes—a real time saver!

THE INTERNET: SURF YOUR WAY TO FINANCIAL INFORMATION

Of course, the time and money savings of e-mail and instant messages is only part of the package. One of the biggest boons to money managers of the lazy persuasion has been the Internet, which can put a dizzying amount of financial information at your fingertips.

The World Wide Web is a huge chunk of the Internet where companies, universities, consumer groups, organizations, news companies, government agencies, and individuals post information on Web sites, free for the taking. With just a click of the mouse, you can download pages of graphics, details, and links to other Web sites. Powerful search engines help you look for topics tailored to your own desires. For example, if you're in the market for a new car, simply search using the words "new car" or "Mercedes" (if you're feeling adventurous). This can save days, weeks, and months that you would have spent in a dusty library, if you had the time and inclination. Many sites are little more than advertisement vehicles.

Want to invest? You can find information on just

about every company and mutual fund. Most companies have their own Web site; even the disciplinary actions of the SEC and National Association of Securities Dealers are just a click away.

Now, let's see just what you can do with your computer to help you manage your money in the least amount of time . . .

MONEY MANAGEMENT

Doing your taxes is just one way you can manage your money on your computer. Intuit, Microsoft, and Meca Software all sell popular financial planning programs, all boasting computerized ledgers that ask you to enter details about checking, savings, and investment transactions. They can automatically update your portfolio, balance your checkbook, and sort your spending into categories. If you bank electronically, you can download your banking transactions into these programs.

Microsoft Money '98 Financial Suite ($29.95 to $54.95) also offers you a goal planner so you can monitor your progress toward long-term goals. Even more fun: You can use the program to connect to the Microsoft investor Web site (http://www.investor.com) for market updates, business news, and stock information (more than 8,000 picks). The screening service costs $9.95, but a six-month free subscription comes with the software.

Intuit's Quicken ($39.95 to $59.95) and Quicken Suite '98 (with special retirement planner) has a goal planner as well that automatically calculates how quickly your savings program will help you reach your long-term

YOU'LL THANK YOURSELF LATER

Ask your bank if it gives Meca Software's Managing Your Money Plus free to customers; it's a spending, savings, and investment planner similar to Quicken and Microsoft Money.

goals. The Deluxe version can connect you to Quicken's Web site (http://www.quicken.com), where you can download the latest stock quotes and mutual fund prices into your portfolio. You can track down the best rates on life and disability insurance and mortgages, and screen 8,540 stocks and 6,000 mutual funds for free.

FILING TAXES THE NO SWEAT, NO FRET WAY!

Those of you who can't bear to stand in line at the post office on April 15 will be thrilled to find out you can file your forms without ever getting up out of your easy chair. You do it by first getting one of the popular tax software packages.

The two most popular packages are TurboTax (and its Macintosh sister, MacInTax) by Intuit (http://www. intuit.com), and Kiplinger Tax Cut by Block Financial Software (http://www.taxcut.com). Both have a range of fun features, and both allow you to transfer data from other financial management software to tax deduction or expense categories.

Both TurboTax ($35 to $50) and Kiplinger Tax Cut ($20; $25 for state version) hold your hand and guide you through an interview process that includes a "refund monitor," automatically changing your bottom line each time you insert an entry. The program enters the data in the proper categories and does the calculations for you. (In addition, Kiplinger displays lines of the tax form as you answer its questions.)

IF YOU'RE SO INCLINED

For more tax-related Internet sites, check out Tax Logic at http://www.taxlogic.com/usatoday.html.

Then the programs check for omissions and flag deductions that you might have forgotten. They compare your deductions and taxes to national statistics on filers in your income bracket, so you can see for yourself if you've gone way overboard in claiming deductions for that five-martini lunch with your brother-in-law.

When everything is done, the programs spit out tax forms for you to mail. You can even file them electronically to the IRS. Done!

MUTUAL FUNDS: A WEALTH OF INFORMATION AT YOUR FINGERTIPS!

If it's mutual funds you're looking for—and these days, most people are—there are several software choices that can help you select funds while you're sitting in your pajamas sipping your morning coffee. These programs are particularly good if you don't have access to the World Wide Web, which posts information on mutual funds as well.

Ascent by Morningstar, Inc. (800-735-0700), offers text and onscreen aids that help you choose mutual funds while minimizing risk. Costs range from $45 for no updates to, $95 for four updates and $195 for a version that updates once a month for a year.

Then there's Mutual Fund Expert, by Steele Systems (800-379-0679), which covers more than 10,000 funds at $50 basic, $107 for quarterly updates, and $220 for monthly updates.

If you're interested in specific stocks held in mutual fund portfolios, the No-Load Analyzer for Windows by

QUICK ⬛ PAINLESS

To decide if you should move from a traditional IRA to a Roth IRA, check out the IRA Analyzer ($9.95) from mutual fund giant T. Rowe Price. Call 800-332-6407 for details.

Value Line (800-284-7607) contains everything the other programs do and also lists up to 50 stocks held in each fund. It costs $95 with quarterly updates.

COMPUTERIZED BROKERAGE: TURN YOUR COMPUTER INTO YOUR ADVISOR

If you're interested in doing your own investing, you may want to check out some of the online brokerage services that have popped up on the Internet recently. Once you set up an account, the service can execute trades on stocks, bonds, mutual funds, and options—often for a per-trade fee of less than $10. Most services will do research (some charge a small amount); for example, Charles Schwab sells company reports for as little as $3. You also can get an up-to-the-minute report of your holdings.

These days, of course, security is a big issue with anyone who makes any sort of financial transaction online. Although most investment companies use encryption software to protect their customers, it's still possible (but very unlikely) that a hacker could get access to your account and make unauthorized trades. The good news: Offline security means that no hacker can transfer assets out of your account, anyway.

Here are a few sites to try:

▪ Discover Brokerage	http://www.discoverbrokerage.com
▪ DLJ Direct	http://www.dljdirect.com
▪ E*Trade	http://www.etrade.com

e.Schwab	http://www.eschwab.com
Lindner Funds	http://www.lindnerfunds.com
Quick & Reilly	http://www.quick-reilly.com
Wall Street Electronica	http://www.wallstreete.com
Waterhouse	http://www.waterhouse.com
Web Street Securities	http://www.webstreetsecurities.com

IF YOU'RE SO
INCLINED

Dive into the Net to make your computer become your at-home advisor, and save both money and time!

Getting Time on Your Side

	The Old Way	The Lazy Way
Buying/selling stock	20 minutes	2 minutes
Checking your bank balance	10 minutes	1 minute
Researching stocks	5 hours	1 hour
Paying bills	3 days	5 minutes
Finding a job	2 days	10 minutes
Keeping in touch	1 week	5 minutes

Who's on First? Finding Expert Financial Help

We've spent all this time talking about financial shortcuts, but of course, the easiest way to manage your money is to hire someone else to do it. In the financial world, there are a wide variety of experts from whom to choose.

Your financial advisor can be your accountant, stockbroker, insurance agent, banker, financial planner—even an attorney or real estate agent. Whomever you choose, a financial advisor can set up a budget, open a life insurance trust, or guide you with retirement planning and take care of your money while you sit by the pool sipping a piña colada.

Plans can be short term. Maybe you want to know how you can arrange a trip to Bora Bora and still afford your alimony payments. It's a better idea, though, to make a plan that encompasses every aspect of your financial situation.

Of course, lots of times you may not need—or want—a complete financial makeover. Who's got the time? No problem! Planners are happy to look at just one or two problems instead of spending days on "the big picture."

Whatever you want, though, your advisor should put your financial plan in writing so you can hold it in your hands, tack it up on your bulletin board, or read it to your friends if you want to. It's much easier to get serious about money if it's all there in black and white. The plan should summarize your goals, mention how much risk you think your heart can stand, describe your current financial condition, and indicate how the advisor will put your plan in action. This way, you know that you both are grounded in some financial reality.

If you're interested in getting some help with your finances, look for a good, qualified planner, not a cheap one. Although there are several types of advisors who won't come to you for a paycheck, nobody works for free. Someone is paying them, and if it's not you it's likely a financial products company looking to sell some investments.

The best way to find investment help is by borrowing a friend's advisor, if you've got friends with financial savvy. If you don't, try contacting a professional organization for their suggestions. Most maintain lists of experts near you.

Once you have a list of names, it's time to start thinking about just what sort of help you're looking for and how you want to pay for it. Remember, the goal is to get someone to work with your money so you don't have to. It pays to find someone top-notch.

COMMISSIONS VERSUS FEES: WHICH WILL GET YOU MORE FOR YOUR MONEY?

When you hire a commission-based planner, you're not really getting a financial "advisor" or "counselor"—you're getting a salesperson. In fact, people who used to call themselves stockbrokers or insurance brokers are now referring to themselves as "financial consultants," which really cloaks the fact that they earn their fees from commissions. It's sort of like a vacuum cleaner salesman calling himself a "home beautification consultant." Would you expect a Hoover rep to tell you how terrific Electrolux cleaners are? The Hoover guy is going to push his Hoovers, and if he mentions the Electrolux at all, it will be to rip it apart.

A fee-based advisor is a financial planner who charges you a percentage of the investments you're buying. The good news: There is no incentive to sell you on investments with high commissions (such as limited partnerships), or to generate lots of transactions as a way of producing more commissions.

However, if the person's income is based on your total amount of assets, he won't want you to do anything that will eat up your investment capital, such as paying down your mortgage, no matter how much sense it might make.

YOU'LL THANK YOURSELF LATER

To find a planner, try calling the Institute of Certified Financial Planners (800-282-7526), International Association for Financial Planning (800-945-4237), National Association of Personal Financial Advisors (800-FEE-ONLY), American Society of CLU/ChFC (800-392-6900), or American Institute of Certified Public Accountants (800-862-4272).

An hourly-based advisor doesn't sell investment products, so you can feel comfortable that any advice you get will be unbiased. You're billed for her time, period. With this expert, what you see is what you get.

So now you know the basic ways that experts are paid. If you want to start managing your money the lazy way, sit back, put your feet up, and hand over your bankbooks to one of these folks:

- Financial planner (CFP, ChFC)
- CPA (Certified Public Accountant)
- Insurance agent
- Private money manager
- Tax preparer
- Stockbroker/financial consultant

FINANCIAL PLANNERS: PAVING YOUR WAY TO FINANCIAL SECURITY

A financial planner is a professional who advises you how to spend and save your money—and often, how to make more money. Some planners define your goals, provide a plan, and then send you to another expert who puts the plan in action. Other planners specialize in buying and selling financial products. Still others will work with you through every stage in the plan.

You'll probably benefit from financial planning if you're getting married, getting divorced, retiring, or doing anything else that can dramatically affect your finances. You may not need a total financial plan, but a review of your situation might make you feel better, and

A COMPLETE WASTE OF TIME

The 3 Worst Things to Do When Getting Financial Help:

1. Hiring someone without checking references.

2. Hiring a tax attorney to answer simple tax questions.

3. Not bothering to read your brokerage statement.

you'd be surprised how often a review can save you time and money. Having a structured financial plan is important to your financial well-being.

Not just anybody can hang out a "financial planner" shingle. Such a designation indicates the person has a business education and at least three years' experience (five years is better).

Planners may work independently, or they may belong to either a local or a national firm. Large firms are known for their trained personnel and access to research, but independent planners often offer more independent advice. The reputation of the planner is what is most important.

Remember that a total financial plan can be expensive, so unless you're already living off the interest of a private trust fund, take it a step at a time. Focus on one aspect of your plan, and then keep going if you are satisfied with the service provided.

IF YOU'RE SO
INCLINED

Use a financial planner to review your situation now and you'll probably find a wealth of options that you never knew existed!

CERTIFIED FINANCIAL PLANNER (CFP): GETTING A LITTLE MORE BACKGROUND

A certified financial planner (CFP) is a financial planner with something extra: The person has earned the CFP designation from the College for Financial Planning in Denver, Colorado, given to those who've passed an exam, had three years' work experience in the field, and completed a two-year program in tax planning, investments, and other aspects of personal finance. It doesn't stop there; CFPs agree to undergo 30 hours of continuing education every two years.

CHARTERED FINANCIAL CONSULTANT (CHFC): WHEN YOU NEED A LITTLE BIT MORE DEFINITION

Financial planners may go in a different direction and earn a Chartered Financial Consultant (ChFC) designation by the American College in Bryn Mawr, Pennsylvania. ChFCs pass 10 courses in financial planning, wealth accumulation, and estate planning, and they must have three years' related work experience and 30 hours of continuing education every two years.

A major difference between the CFPs and ChFCs is that ChFCs don't have to take a 10-hour exam, and their training allows them to specialize in a particular area of financial planning, such as insurance or investments.

PERSONAL FINANCIAL SPECIALIST (PFS): A LITTLE BIT EXTRA

A PFS is a certified public account (CPA) who is designated as a Personal Financial Specialist from the American Institute of Certified Public Accountants. This title is given to CPAs who have passed a six-hour test and who have three years' experience in financial planning. Many states allow only CPAs to advertise themselves as an "accountants." Non-CPA accountants get around this by advertising "accounting services," "bookkeeping," or "tax preparation."

QUICK ⬤ PAINLESS

It's a good idea to choose a planner with one of these sets of initials (PFS, CFC, CFP, or ChFC) plus a degree in accounting, marketing, economics, business, or finance; and three to five years of financial planning experience.

MONEY MANAGER: WHEN YOU'VE MADE IT BIG, THIS IS WHO YOU SHOULD CALL

A money manager is a kind of financial planner for people with a lot of money who manages it so you don't have to, handling your funds and buying and selling stocks and bonds on your behalf. A money manager is a financial advisor who has total discretion to handle the funds you want to have managed: You hand over the money and kiss your worries goodbye. Of course, hiring a money manager means you also hand over a significant salary, which is why money managers stick to wealthy clients.

TAX PREPARER—OR, GETTING SOMEONE ELSE TO CRUNCH THOSE NUMBERS!

Yes, you can sit down with those tax forms, your receipts, and a big bottle of Maalox and do your taxes yourself. But if you're looking for the easy way, you'll think about hiring someone else for this job. Should that be a tax preparation chain, an enrolled agent, a tax attorney, or a CPA?

The tax chains are fast and in March and April, they are very busy. They usually file returns electronically, which means you'll get your refund quicker; some chains offer "instant refunds." (This is really a loan made against your anticipated federal income tax refund—but beware: The fees are high.)

A COMPLETE WASTE OF TIME

The 3 Worst Things to Do at Tax Time:

1. Put it off until April 13th.

2. Leave it to your dog.

3. Assume you have to do it all yourself.

IF YOU'RE SO

INCLINED

To find an enrolled agent, call the National Association of Enrolled Agents' 24-hour hotline at 800-424-4339. They will send you a list of three agents in your area.

National chains are convenient, and they're helpful for those without lots of time on their hands. The problem is that the agent you work with this year may well not be there next year. You don't get personal service; if you are audited, a chain agent can go with you, but he can't go in your place.

An enrolled agent is licensed by the government to represent you before the IRS. Enrolled agents aren't CPAs, but they must have passed a rigorous two-day exam or worked for five years in a tax-related capacity. If you ever have problems and need to deal with the IRS, an enrolled agent is there to help you.

A tax attorney knows a lot about taxes, but no tax attorney can prepare your tax return. If you have some tax questions, both a tax attorney and a CPA can help you, but only the CPA can file your return—and the CPA is much cheaper. You'd hire a tax attorney if you got in serious trouble with the IRS and had to go to tax court.

If you're in an audit and the questions get tough—and you don't know the answers—you have the right to adjourn the meeting at any time. And if you're asked about issues not related to your original notice, you can ask for extra time to get the right documentation.

CERTIFIED PUBLIC ACCOUNTANTS (CPAS): WHO THEY REALLY ARE

A Certified Public Accountant (CPA) is licensed by the state (an "accountant" is not) and has a college degree or equivalent (some states now require graduate work as well). CPAs must pass a comprehensive exam in accountancy, taxation, and business law, and work for two years under another CPA's supervision. They have a rigorous continuing education requirement of 80 hours every two years. You can find a good CPA by contacting the American Institute of Certified Public Accountants, 1211 Avenue of the Americas, New York, NY 10036.

BANK ADVISORS: HOW YOUR BANK CAN HELP YOU

There are two types of bank advisors. The customer service representatives are those front-line folks who open your savings and checking accounts, sell you a Certificate of Deposit (CD), and so on. They know about their bank's products, and while they can be helpful, they are limited in what they can advise.

Some financial advisors are also personal bankers. Personal bankers provide personal, consolidated services. They can lower fees charged to your account, and they can verify that you are getting the best account for the amount of money you have invested. A personal banker can expedite loans and consolidate services for you.

Your banker also can act as your broker. As the investment business changes, everybody is wearing different hats. Insurance agents sell investments, bankers sell investments, and insurance brokers sell insurance and CDs. It becomes difficult to know who does what.

Your bank can have a brokerage arm (a subsidiary) that will help you buy an investment. Many banks that don't have such a brokerage arm have employees who can sell annuities and mutual funds through an outside service.

YOU'LL THANK YOURSELF LATER

For a full list of your rights during an audit, check IRS Publication #1. You can download it from the IRS Web site at http://www.irs. ustreas.gov on the World Wide Web.

QUICK IN PAINLESS

Comparison shop for cost. Having your banker act as a broker can have benefits for the lazy money manager. You can transfer money to pay for trades directly from your bank checking account and you can deal locally.

ANNUITY SERVICE FINANCIAL PLANNERS: NOT ALWAYS THE BEST CHOICE

Annuity service planners are simply brokers for various annuity companies. Why put all your financial eggs in one type of package? Many annuities have performed well in the recent past, but by limiting yourself to an annuity provider, you are almost assured of being told that an annuity is the answer to your financial needs. In fact, it may not be the best answer. Annuity companies pay their salespersons on a commission basis, which can be as high as 8 percent of the value of the funds you buy.

RETIREMENT PLANNING EXPERTS: HELPING YOU NOW FOR LATER ON

There are certainly questions you need to answer as you approach retirement. For example, should you take a lump sum payment at retirement to roll the funds into your own IRA account? Financial planners have software to help you make the decision, so you shouldn't need a retirement expert. If you do use a retirement specialist, make sure you know how he or she will be paid.

FINANCIAL PLANNING SEMINARS: THE PLUSSES AND MINUSES

Taking free seminars on financial planning can be a good way to learn about the investment field and can save you time and money in the long run. However, you need to understand that there's a hidden agenda here: These seminars are the planner's way of attracting potential clients. After you have reviewed the planner's education, experience, and fees, it's up to you whether you want to work with that planner any further.

Finance classes at local colleges are often taught by instructors, but these folks, too, are really brokers or financial planners trolling for clients. You probably won't get many specifics here, but you'll be encouraged to "see" the instructor after class (read "hire" here). Sometimes colleges hire these people as instructors because they know they want to sell financial products, and therefore the school doesn't have to pay them as much.

Of course, there are also ethical instructors at these classes who will be there to teach, not to solicit clients. You can separate the wheat from the chaff by the fact that ethical instructors will discourage their students from hiring them.

INSURANCE AGENTS AS FINANCIAL PLANNERS: YOU GET WHAT YOU PAY FOR

Insurance agents are paid primarily on a commission basis from the insurance products they sell. An

IF YOU'RE SO INCLINED

Take a seminar and in a few hours learn more than you might have been able to in one week!

experienced, knowledgeable agent can give you details on your policies, death benefits, premiums, and so on. But wake up and smell the coffee: If you get general financial advice from your insurance agent, chances are that insurance will somehow figure into the solution. An insurance agent works directly with the insurance company and usually is an employee of the company.

ATTORNEYS: WHAT THEY MIGHT SAVE YOU

You might not think of an attorney as a financial advisor, but a good lawyer can save your family a lot of money in your total estate plan. She can negotiate prenuptial agreements, divorce settlements, adoptions, custody matters, and wills. Remember that attorneys charge on an hourly basis and that clock is always ticking, so don't waste time on the phone in idle chitchat.

STOCKBROKERS: IS THIS WHAT YOU REALLY NEED?

If you want to stick your toe into the stock market, you'll need a stockbroker to buy the stock and make trades. If you don't want the hassle of hiring one, you also can buy stock directly through the Internet, although you're still really using a broker. (See Chapter 16 on computerized money management.) You can choose between a full-service stockbroker or a discount broker, depending on how much you want to pay and what kind of service you need.

IF YOU'RE SO INCLINED

You can get information about your broker from a CRUD (Central Registration Depository) report: his work history, how long he's been registered, and whether he has been sued, paid damages, or convicted of a crime. Call the National Association of Securities Dealers at 800-289-9999.

A full-service stockbroker will recommend which stock you should purchase and what the long-term investment strategies and risks are. He or she will check over your portfolio, provide periodic updates of your account's performance, and send you research material about investments.

None of this comes cheap, of course. A stockbroker will charge you a commission on each transaction you make. (Remember, if you sell one stock and buy another, you pay two commissions.) While your interests should be considered first, the truth is that the brokers are required to sell. In today's world, the person who sells most is considered the best broker. Brokerage houses demand a certain level of commission income, and many firms have bonuses for overall sales production, as well as trips and gifts for exceptional sales. In addition to forking over a fee each time you buy or sell, you'll be paying for:

- Postage and handling
- Annual account fees
- Transferring the account to another brokerage house

DISCOUNT BROKERS: PAY LESS, AND GET LESS

A discount broker is a great choice for someone who picks her own stocks, but might not be the best choice for lazy money managers who don't want to think too much about finance. This is a no-frills service, which

QUICK ⬛ PAINLESS

For an easy way to find a deep discount broker, try:

- Jack White & Co. (800-431-3500)
- Lombard (800-566-2273)
- Brown & Co. (800-822-2021)

means you will get research information but you won't get recommendations about buying or selling, or general investment advice. You are paying for transactions, though you'll pay about 45 percent to 70 percent less than most full-service firms charge.

Then you have your deep discount brokers, who are even cheaper than discount brokers. With these folks, you really are on your own; you get no investment research material, and you may not be able to buy the full range of products. Deep discount brokers make their money on volume, so don't expect your expert to get chummy or offer investment advice.

Online brokerage services allow you to set up an account to execute trades on stocks, bonds, mutual funds, and options—often for a per-trade fee of less than $10. Most services will do research (some charge a small amount); for example, Charles Schwab sells company reports for as little as $3. You also can get an up-to-the-minute report of your holdings.

Here are a few sites to try:

- Discover Brokerage   http://www.discoverbrokerage.com
- DLJ Direct   http://www.dljdirect.com
- E*Trade   http://www.etrade.com
- e.Schwab   http://www.eschwab.com
- Lindner Funds   http://www.lindnerfunds.com
- Quick & Reilly   http://www.quick-reilly.com

YOU'LL THANK YOURSELF LATER

Before choosing an online brokerage, visit Gomez Advisors' Web site (http://www.gomezadvisors.com). This Boston firm ranks online trading services according to cost, ease of use, customer confidence, onsite resources, availability of other services, and appropriateness for investors.

- Wall Street Electronica — http://www.wallstreete.com
- Waterhouse — http://www.waterhouse.com
- Web Street Securities — http://www.webstreetsecurities.com

QUICK 𝗻 PAINLESS

Check out these Web sites before choosing a brokerage and you'll ensure the right decision for your needs.

Getting Time on Your Side

	The Old Way	**The Lazy Way**
Filing your taxes	2 days	20 minutes
Planning your finances	1 day	45 minutes
Handling stock	2 hours	5 minutes
Choosing a brokerage firm	1 week	2 hours
Comparing brokers	1 week	10 minutes
Choosing a CPA	2 weeks	2 days

More Lazy Stuff

How to Get Someone Else to Do It

Let's face it: If you barely have time to brush your teeth in the morning and feed the dog at night before falling into bed, how on earth are you going to find the time to manage your investments, track your spending, save your tax-deductible receipts, remember to send in quarterly payments . . . whew! You get a headache just thinking about it.

The fastest, simplest, and easiest way to deal with all things financial is simply to pay someone else to take care of them. After all, you hire the neighborhood kids to wash your car, mow your lawn, and feed your cat when you go on vacation. You may have a cleaning lady come in once a week, somebody tune your piano, and someone else spread chemicals on your lawn.

Why mess with your money if somebody out there can do it faster, easier, better—and maybe make you more money than you could yourself? Yes, it sure makes sense to hire some type of financial advisor.

But lots of people feel very vulnerable when they hand over the reins of their financial empire. After all, what's the worst thing the neighborhood kid could do to your cat? Reach for the Friskies instead of the

Purina? But a financial mistake, however well intentioned, can have much more serious repercussions.

Whomever you choose as a financial advisor, for whatever specific duties, should be absolutely the best trained, most honest person you can afford. But oddly enough, people often spend more time investigating their hairdresser than they do a financial advisor. Often, people choose a money manager simply by running a finger down the yellow pages.

Well, no more! Since we already know you don't have much time, we've provided a list of handy questions you can take along when you interview your potential money manager.

- What are your educational background, your college major, and your degrees?

- Have you qualified as a certified financial planner (CFP) or a chartered financial consultant (ChFC)? Are you a member of the Registry of Financial Planning Practitioners?

- Are you a member of a professional financial planning association?

- How long have you been in business?

- What sort of continuing education in finance do you pursue?

- May I have some client references?

- How many clients in my financial bracket do you have? May I see a copy of a plan you've prepared for someone (no names, of course) in a situation similar to mine?

- Will you personally work on my plan?
- What ongoing help will you give me to put my plan in action?
- Have you ever been disciplined by a professional or regulatory governing body?
- How are you paid?
- What are your charges and how do you earn them? (for fee-only planners)

If You Really Want More, Read These

Abentrod, Susan. *10 Minute Guide to Beating Debt*. New York: Macmillan General Reference, 1996.

Baldwin, Ben G. *The Complete Book of Insurance: The Consumer's Guide to Insuring Your Life, Health, Property & Income*. Chicago: Probus Publishing, 1996.

Baldwin, Ben G. *New York Insurance Investment Adviser: Achieving Financial Security for You and Your Family Through Today's Insurance Products*. Chicago: Irwin Professional Publishing, 1994.

Beth, Joseph M. *Life Insurance: A Consumer's Handbook*. Bloomington, IN: Indiana University Press, 1985.

Bierman, Todd, and David Masten. *The Fix Your Credit Workbook: A Step by Step Guide to a Lifetime of Great Credit*. New York: St. Martin's Press, 1998.

Bilker, Scott. *Credit Card & Debt Management: A Step-by-Step How-To Guide for Organizing and Saving Money on Interest Payments*. Barnegat, NJ: Press One, 1996.

Blue, Ron, and Charles R. Swindoll. *Master Your Money: A Step-by-Step Plan for Financial Freedom*. New York: Thomas Nelson Publishers, 1997.

Breuel, Brian H. *The Complete Idiot's Guide to Buying Insurance & Annuities*. New York: Alpha Books, 1996.

Cronin, Mary J. *Banking and Finance on the Internet*. New York: Van Nostrand Reinhold, 1997.

Editors, Consumer Reports. *How to Buy a Condo or Co-op*. Consumer Reports Books, 1996.

Enteen, Robert. *Health Insurance: How to Get It, Keep It or Improve What You've Got*. New York: Demos Vermande, 1996.

Epstein, Robert. *Maximizing Your Health Insurance Benefits: A Consumer's Guide to New and Traditional Plans*. Westport, CT: Praeger Publishers, 1997.

Ernst, et al. *Ernst & Young's Tax Saver's Guide 1998* (Annual). New York: John Wiley & Sons, 1997.

Feinberg, Andrew. *Downsize Your Debt: How to Take Control of Your Personal Finances*. New York: Penguin Books, USA, 1993.

Fisher, Sarah Young, and Carol Turkington. *Everything You Need to Know About Money and Investing: A Financial Expert Answers the 1001 Most Frequently Asked Questions About Money*. Paramus, NJ: Prentice Hall, 1998.

Fitch, Thomas. *Dictionary of Banking Terms*, 3rd Ed. Hauppauge, NY: Barron's Educational Series, 1997.

Friedman, Jack P. *Dictionary of Real Estate Terms*. Hauppauge, NY: Barron's Educational Series, 1997.

Friedman, Jack P., PhD, and Jack C. Friedman, PhD. *Keys to Investing in Real Estate*. Hauppauge, New York: Barron's Educational Series, 1993.

Garner, Robert J. (Ed.). *Ernst & Young's Total Financial Planner*. New York: John Wiley & Sons, 1996.

Garner, Robert J., et al. *Ernst & Young's Retirement Planning Guide: Take Care of Your Finances Now, and They'll Take Care of You Later*. New York: John Wiley & Sons, 1997.

Gelb, Eric P. *10 Minute Guide to Annual Reports and Propectuses*. New York: Macmillan General Reference, 1996.

Glink, Ilyce R. *100 Questions Every First-Time Home Buyer Should Ask: With Answers from Top Brokers from Around the Country*. New York: Times Books, 1994.

Goetze, Jean G. *Long Term Care*. Chicago: Dearborn Financial Publishing, 1997.

Gold, Laura Maery, and Dan Post. *Invest On Line: Do It Yourself and Keep More of What You Earn*. New York: Macmillan, 1997.

Goldberg, Seymour. *J.K. Lasser's How to Pay Less Tax on Your Retirement Savings*, 2nd Ed. New York: Macmillan General Reference, 1997.

H&R Block. *H&R Block 1998 Income Tax Guide*. Columbus, OH: Fireside, 1997.

Heady, Robert, and Christy Heady. *The Complete Idiot's Guide to Managing Your Money*. New York: Macmillan General Reference, 1995.

Hymer, Dian Davis. *Starting Out: The Complete Home Buyer's Guide*. San Francisco: Chronicle Books, 1997.

Lasser, J.K. *Your Income Tax 1998*. New York: Macmillan General Reference, 1997.

Lieberman, Gail, and Alan Lavine. *Improving Your Credit and Reducing Your Debt*. New York: John Wiley & Sons, 1994.

Lilke, Sheryl. *Understanding Personal Auto Insurance*. Chicago: Dearborn Trade, 1995.

Lockwood, Georgene Muller. *The Complete Idiot's Guide to Organizing Your Life*. New York: Alpha Books, 1997.

Loungo, Tracy. *10 Minute Guide to Household Budgeting*. New York: Macmillan General Reference, 1997.

Lowell, James. *Investing from Scratch: A Handbook for the Young Investor*. New York: Penguin Books, USA, 1997.

McCormally, Kevin (ed.). *Kiplinger Cut Your Taxes, 1998*, 8th Ed. Richmond, VA: Kiplinger Books, 1998.

McCullough, Bonnie Runyon. *Bonnie's Household Budget Book: The Essential Workbook for Getting Control of Your Money*. New York: St. Martin's Press, 1996.

McNaughton, Deborah. *Insider's Guide to Managing Your Credit: How to Establish, Maintain, Repair and Protect Your Credit*. Chicago: Dearborn Trade, 1997.

Mayer, Andy. *Where Does All the Money Go?: Taking Control of Your Personal Expenses.* New York: W.W. Norton & Son, 1992.

Merritt Editors. *Hassle Free Health Coverage: How to Buy the Right Medical Insurance, Cheaply and Effectively.* Santa Monica, CA: Merritt Co., 1998.

Merritt Editors. *How to Insure Your Car: A Step by Step Guide to Buying the Coverage You Need at Prices You Can Afford.* Santa Monica, CA: Merritt Co., 1996.

Merritt Editors. *How to Insure Your Home: A Step by Step Guide to Buying the Coverage You Need at Prices You Can Afford.* Santa Monica, CA: Merritt Co., 1996.

Morris, Kenneth M., et al. *The Wall Street Journal Guide to Planning Your Financial Future.* Columbus, OH: Fireside, 1995.

Morris, Kenneth M., and Alan M. Siegel. *The Wall Street Journal Guide to Understanding Money & Investing.* New York: Simon & Schuster, 1994.

Morris, Kenneth M., and Alan M. Siegel. *The Wall Street Journal Guide to Understanding Your Personal Finances.* Columbus, OH: Lightbulb Press, 1997.

O'Hara, Shelly. *The Complete Idiot's Guide to Buying & Selling a Home.* New York: Macmillan General Reference, 1996.

Orman, Suze, and Linda Mead. *You've Earned It, Don't Lose It: Mistakes You Can't Afford to Make When You Retire.* Boston: Newmarket Press, 1997.

Pearl, Diane, and Ellie Williams Clinton. *The Smart Woman's Guide to Spending, Saving and Managing Money*. New York: HarperCollins Publishers, 1994.

Quinn, Jane Bryant. *Making the Most of Your Money*. New York: Simon & Schuster, 1997.

Rowland, Mary. *A Commonsense Guide to Your 401(K)*. Princeton: Bloomberg Press, 1997.

Rubin, Harvey W. *Dictionary of Insurance Terms* (Barron's Business Guides). Hauppauge, NY: Barron's Educational Series, 1995.

Schwab, Charles R. *Charles Schwab's Guide to Financial Independence: Simple Solutions for Busy People*. New York: Crown Publications, 1998.

Shenkman, Martin M. *Estate Planning: Step-by-Step* (Barron's Legal-Ease Series). Hauppauge, NY: Barron's Educational Series, 1997.

Slott, Ed. *Your Tax Questions Answered 1998: A CPA With Over Twenty Years of Experience Answers the Most Commonly Asked Questions*. Plymouth, MI: Plymouth Press Ltd., 1997.

Spare, Anthony, and Paul Ciotti. *Last Chance Financial Planning Guide: It's Not Too Late to Plan Your Retirement If You Start Now*. Rocklin, CA: Prima Publishing, 1997.

Steinbach, Robert. *Out of Debt: How to Clean Up Your Credit and Balance Your Budget While Avoiding Bankruptcy*. Holbrook, MA: Adams Publishing, 1989.

Tinney, Diane, et al. *Organize Your Finances with Quicken Deluxe 98: In a Weekend*. Rocklin, CA: Prima Publishing, 1998.

Tyson, Eric, et al. *Understanding Personal Umbrella Insurance*. Chicago: Dearborn Trade, 1995.

Walsh, James. *What Do You Mean It's Not Covered?: A Guide to Understanding What Your Insurance Does—and Doesn't—Cover*. Santa Monica, CA: Merritt Co., 1995.

Webb, Martha, and Sarah Parsons Zackheim. *Dress Your House for Success: 5 Fast, Easy Steps to Selling Your House, Apartment or Condo for the Highest Possible Price*. New York: Three Rivers Publishing, 1997.

If You Don't Know What It Means, Look Here

Adjusted gross income (AGI) A method used to calculate income tax that is computed by subtracting the allowable deductions from gross income.

Aggressive growth fund A mutual fund that has a primary investment objective of seeking capital gains.

Amortization Reducing the principal of a loan by regular payments.

Annuity A contract between an insurance company and an individual in which the company agrees to provide an income for a specific period, in exchange for money.

Balanced mutual fund A mutual fund that has a primary investment objective of purchasing a combination of stocks and bonds. Such funds tend to be less volatile than stock-only funds.

Bear market A sharply declining market.

Beneficiary The person who is named to receive the proceeds from an investment vehicle. A beneficiary can be an individual, a company, or an organization.

Blue chip A solid-performing common stock with a sterling reputation based on consistent long-term earnings despite market fluctuations, 25 years or more of paying quarterly cash dividends, and leadership in solid industry with an expectation for continued success.

Bond An instrument on which the issuer promises to pay the investor a specified amount of interest, and to repay the principal at maturity.

Bull market A stock market that is rising sharply.

Capital gain The difference between the cost of an asset and its higher selling price. Tax on this gain is usually due when the asset is sold.

Certificate of deposit (CD) An investment available from a bank that pays a fixed rate of return for a specified period of time.

Common stock Shares of ownership in a corporation.

Compound interest Interest figured on the principal and the interest that has built up during the preceding period. Compound interest may be figured daily, monthly, quarterly, semiannually, or annually.

Consumer Price Index A measure of the relative cost of living for a family of four compared with a base year.

Dividend The proportion of net earnings paid to stockholders by a corporation. Dividends are usually fixed in preferred stock; dividends from common stock vary as the company's performance shifts.

Equity The value of your ownership in property or securities. Your equity in your home is the difference between the current market value of the home and the money you still owe the bank on the mortgage.

Financial advisor A professional who helps people arrange and coordinate their financial affairs.

401(k) plan A retirement plan to which you can contribute a portion of your current salary (usually before taxes). Contributions can grow tax-deferred until they are withdrawn upon retirement.

Government securities Bonds, bills, or notes sold by the federal government to raise money.

Gross income Income that includes all potentially taxable income, including wages, salary, dividends, interest, retirement plan distributions, and so on. Gross income is the starting point in determining tax liability.

Growth fund A mutual fund that invests in common stocks that grow faster than normal. Growth funds are long-term investments.

Individual Retirement Account (IRA) A retirement savings plan in which you can contribute up to $2,000 annually that can grow tax-deferred until withdrawn at retirement age. Contributions may or may not be tax deductible depending on income level and participation in other retirement plans.

Inflation An increase in the price of goods and services over time, representing the decreased buying power.

Interest The cost of borrowing money.

Liquidity Your ability to convert your assets into cash without significant loss.

Money market fund A mutual fund that specializes in short-term securities (such as Treasury bills). Money market funds are very safe and offer slightly more interest than a traditional bank savings account.

Municipal bond fund A mutual fund that invests in municipal bonds; you receive dividends that are usually exempt from federal income tax.

Municipal bonds Obligations of states, cities, towns, school districts, and public authorities; interest paid on munis are usually tax-exempt.

Mutual funds An investment that pools money and invests in portfolio of stocks, bonds, options, or money market securities. Mutual funds are diversified and professionally managed.

Portfolio Total assets held by an investor.

Preferred stock A class of stock with a claim on the company's earnings before payment is made on the common stock, if the company declares a dividend.

Treasury bond A U.S. government long-term security with a maturity above five years.

Treasury stock Stock issued by a company and later reacquired.

Trust A form of property ownership in which the legal title to the property is held by someone (the "trustee") for the benefit of someone else (the "beneficiary").

Will A document that recites how a person's property should be distributed after death. It also can be used to name an executor of the estate and a person to serve as the guardian of minor children.

Yield Also known as return. The dividends or interest paid by a company are expressed as a percent of the current price (or if you own the security, as the original price). You can calculate the return on a stock by dividing the total of dividends paid in the preceding 12 months by the current price (or if you're the owner, the original price).

It's Time for Your Reward

So you've put your finances in order, found the bank that's just right for you, streamlined your credit, and begun to prepare for your future financial needs. That's a lot of work! But you did it *The Lazy Way,* so here are some lazy rewards to give yourself as you continue to Handle Your Money The Lazy Way!

Reward Table

Once You've Done This. . .	Reward Yourself. . .
Organized your important papers	Collapse in the hammock
Made a will	Take a pastry break
Set up a mutual fund for your child	Read a good book
Figured out how much life insurance you need	Go rent a video
Checked on your Social Security benefits	Get an ice-cream cone

Once You've Done This. . .	Reward Yourself. . .
Opened a 401(k), an IRA, or a mutual fund	Buy yourself a treat
Started saving for your child's college education	Take a night out with your spouse
Made sure you have enough homeowner's insurance	Call up an old friend
Checked your credit report	Take a weekend trip

Where to Find What You're Looking For

Now you can do these tasks, too!

The Lazy Way™

Starting to think there are a few more of life's little tasks that you've been putting off? Don't worry—we've got you covered. Take a look at all of *The Lazy Way* books available. Just imagine—you can do almost anything *The Lazy Way!*

Clean Your House The Lazy Way
By Barbara H. Durham
0-02-862649-4

Cook Your Meals The Lazy Way
By Sharon Bowers
0-02-862644-3

Care for Your Home The Lazy Way
By Terry Meany
0-02-862646-X

Train Your Dog The Lazy Way
By Andrea Arden
0-87605180-8

Take Care of Your Car The Lazy Way
By Michael Kennedy and Carol Turkington
0-02-862647-8

Learn Spanish The Lazy Way
By Vivian Isaak and Bogumila Michalewicz
0-02-862650-8

additional titles on the back!

Build Your Financial Future The Lazy Way

By Terry Meany

0-02-862648-6

Shed Some Pounds The Lazy Way

By Annette Cain and Becky Cortopassi-Carlson

0-02-862999-X

Organize Your Stuff The Lazy Way

By Toni Ahlgren

0-02-863000-9

Feed Your Kids Right The Lazy Way

By Virginia Van Vynckt

0-02-863001-7

Cut Your Spending The Lazy Way

By Leslie Haggin

0-02-863002-5

Stop Aging The Lazy Way

By Judy Myers, Ph.D.

0-02-862793-8

Get in Shape The Lazy Way

By Annette Cain

0-02-863010-6

Learn French The Lazy Way

By Christophe Desmaison

0-02-863011-4

Learn Italian The Lazy Way

By Gabrielle Euvino

0-02-863014-9

Keep Your Kids Busy The Lazy Way

By Barbara Nielsen and Patrick Wallace

0-02-863013-0